EMERALD REFLECTIONS

A South Seattle Emerald Anthology

edited by

MARCUS HARRISON GREEN

THIRD
PLACE
PRESS

It's Happening Here, It's Happening There, by Jeanne Morel has been previously published in *Raven Chronicles* ; *After Several Sharp Caws in Succession,* by Martha Silano has been previously published in *The Fourth River*

Edited by Marcus Harrison Green

Cover art: ©2016 Victor Straube

Book and cover design: Vladimir Verano, Third Place Press

Published in the United States by Third Place Press

in collaboration with

South Seattle Emerald

ISBN: 978-1-60944-109-8
Library of Congress Control Number: 2016958274

southseattleemerald.com

thirdplacepress.com

CONTENTS

ART

_⌇_

PROSE

_⌇_

INTRODUCTION

༄

The New Harlem…a neo–Athens…the Mumbai of the west. How do you describe the south end of the city of Seattle?

The richness of culture and ethnic diversity bursting from its borders is unparalleled anywhere else in America. From restaurants where Tagalog hums over the sounds of street cars along Rainer Avenue to coffee shops where Ethiopian baristas serve a blend of Harrar, its powerful aroma of blueberries drifting up the nostrils of passersby, who will later on flood into music lounges, adding their personal hue to a mixture of complexions, genders, and creeds; all of them housed under one ceiling, congregated in collective experience.

South Seattle is the roof under which this country's most lusted-after vision flourishes. A dream where myriad backgrounds, orientations and life paths engage in a common cause: seeking to strive together, aspire together and co-exist authentically with one another.

Growing up in a community with three of our country's most diverse zip codes, I was spoiled by a belief that the rest of America mimicked this community's behavior. Such childlike naiveté soon evaporated when I encountered the rest of our world, only increasing my affection for Seattle's South End.

And no, we as a community and a people are not perfect. We have our challenges and issues as is intrinsic to any collection of human beings.

But also intrinsic to this community, is its originality birthed from an aggregation of imagination that can only be produced by the fusion of dozens of world cultures learning, conversing, and aspiring together.

This "human gumbo," as my grandmother Hilliard would often tell me, delighting your soul's palette with its dash of seasonings and spices, from all over the world, contributing to the extraordinary flavor of one delicious dish.

You now hold in your hands a sampling of that entrée, prepared by poets, artists and writers from an aggregation of imagination found in South Seattle's neighborhoods of Skyway, Mount Baker, Rainier Beach, Hillman City, Beacon Hill, Columbia City and Othello to name but a few.

Their words provide you with an exquisite taste of America's living mosaic.

A living mosaic I'm still uncertain how to truly describe, other than what I've affectionately called it for the majority of my life: home.

EMERALD

REFLECTIONS

I.

Poetry

PAULOWNIA TOMENTOSA

by Paul Nelson

His "Good Day!" was always overcast. - Ramon Gomez de la Serna

& yes, he was from Seattle. & yes, the sun was shining that particular Friday in the season of lilac blossoms and a full bloom Empress Tree, Princess Tree, *Paulownia tomentosa*, stolen from central and western China but an invader here loving the lack of competition for what sun there is, shaping purple hanging bell blossoms and *leaves in whorls of three*. We sit under it, take fotos, are there if we think about it, Lakewood Park.

        & by *good day* he meant, in Seattle nice, courtesy and not much else, will wait for your street crossing, will not honk, "a city of the mind … a city of geeks. People here … totally blow you off" the newcomer'd say in The Times. But not at the stop sign beyond the Empress Tree. Not at the four way stop where *you go no you go no you go* & the guy from Chicago goes knowing your M.O., knowing driving the car "is personality enshrined."

        & overhead's a helicopter shopping for dark-skinned shooting suspects & here the "anti-capitalism May Day riots" only 3 businesses w/ busted windows & here a view of deep Elliott Bay azul under snow-capped Olympics seeking a hearing. *Good day*, always overcast, always an undertone, somewhere the intimacy's obscured. Some know the names of dogs at the dog park but not the ones the other side of the leash. Not the neighbor's name or wife, but their latté order or wifi-signal & how much in their compost bin. Is it the weather? Topography? It is a "social script that leads to alienation" but Emmett Watson didn't want you here anyway and we can't make a left on Denny at 1:40 in the afternoon & bike-riders forego single file just to hack at you & your humongous carbon footprint. In Slaughter I once saw a yard sign that said simply: "Vote No!" Can whip it out for any election.

Vote No, democracy easy as yard signs & being against. (Just put a line through it.) Easy as stopping for one pedestrian or take a pill or cut it out, or the bombing starts in 5 minutes or the settler prehension a century after the perimeter's secured.

           & yes, the sun shines that particular Friday the season of late magnolia blossoms, of English Heather, or Scotch Broom petals sticking their heads out of leaves this side the highway, season of lilac blossoms & the full bloom Empress Tree, Princess Tree.

> *Paulownia tomentosa,*
> stolen from western China
> but just an invader here
> like you & me.

GHOSTS

By George Draffan

Every mile we came south the price went down. Our friends were dubious. Wasn't it dangerous? Not really. It was fantastic — a wild, rich mixture of old and new from Europe and Asia and Africa and Latin America. A meeting place of nature and city, language and culture, wealth and poverty, history and the future.

Lushootseed (Salish) people had been here for thousands of years, living in cedar longhouses along the shores of Lake Washington, calling themselves Dkhw'Duw'Absh (Duwamish) and hah-choo-AHBSH (People of the Large Lake). They had camps at Brighton Beach and Pritchard Island and at Bryn Mawr, below Skyway.

When Vancouver sailed into Elliott Bay in the big ships, the boy Si'ahl (Sealth, or Seattle) saw them. Si'ahl made friends with Doc Maynard, but Owhi and Leschi put up a fight, and most of the Salish who weren't felled by disease or violence were rounded up and confined to small places.

The ancient trees were cut for planks and cabins and houses, or simply burned to make room for crops. Guy Phinney built a sawmill at the foot of Charles Street (now the Leschi neighborhood). David and Walter Graham bought a couple hundred acres and planted orchards, and English immigrants bought some parcels to subdivide, and named the area Brighton Beach after a fashionable English resort.

The Rainier Avenue Electric Railway came from downtown to reach Columbia City in 1891 and Renton five years later. Si'ahl's daughter Kikisoblu (Angeline) died in 1896, and within a few more years Columbia City, Rainier Beach, and Brighton Beach were all annexed into the city of Seattle.

Bailey Peninsula became Seward Park, a jewel in the Olmsted Brothers' Emerald Necklace. The Park still has ancient trees, eagle nests, and native plants and animals.

Italians settled, planting fruit orchards and vegetable gardens, and named the place Garlic Gulch. Borracchini's grocery, founded in 1923, is still here, selling pasta and wine and decorated cakes. The plum trees are still here too, abandoned and overgrown and still prolific.

Low-income housing projects at Rainier Vista, Seward Park Estates, and Holly Park were built in the 1940s. African-Americans, forbidden from buying in many Seattle neighborhoods, moved into the Rainier Valley. Brighton Beach and Seward Park became a center for Seattle's Jewish community, with three synagogues and some 90 percent of the city's Orthodox Jewish population. In the 1970s and 80s, Asian immigrants and refugees. In the 1990s, Africans. In the 2000s, Euros from the North End looking for an affordable house. Abandoned orchards overrun by blackberry and ivy are being cleared for million-dollar mansions.

When we moved in, we removed the iron bars from the windows, and planted them in the garden for the vines to climb. Twenty years later, many of the retired folks that were living here have died or moved on, and we're practically the elders on the block, except for the ghosts of salmon, ghosts of ancient trees, ghosts of settlers from around the world, dwelling on the shores of Lake Washington in the southeast corner of the Emerald City.

WALK WOMAN WALK

by Monique Franklin

Walk Woman Walk
Walk that shoulder jiving
neck noose untying walk
Walk that tape poppin'
flip it over and keep boppin' walk
Walk like you sho nuff know the way to freedom

Walk like you never needed a thing but your heart and soul strut
your face saying —
"watch me I got it, watch me I got it
Heeeey!
I got Soul and I 'm super bad"

Cause even in super bad times
You don't let your tape drag tired feet
you live
to wiggle the funk between your toes
When you're lost
You reach for that pen light
And continue
To write neon prose
Reminding yourself of what you already know
"Everybody's got a little light under the sun"
So you can just stroll
"Ha da da dee da hada hada da da
Oh"

Walk woman walk
Like your ideas defy gravity
you are what you think
you stay grounded but not held down by defeat
walk like the clouds are outfitted in your ink
your best lines inscribed in metallic silver streaks

Walk woman walk
Like your looking for something loud like the yell Oh! Of the Sun Hollerin'
"We are people of the mighty
Mighty people of the sun"
Walk like you are the ONE.
Your inner soul pouring out of every fuse on your face
Meander like your slow is Flo Jo winning the race
While your intentions travels at light speeds
Your actions keep pace

Walk woman walk
Like Saturn just purposed
A ring for your love and six more just because
Walk
Like the lyrics of life
Are painted on dice
That always land sevens in your palms

Like your right hand
is a map of the streets that never dead end
and your left is a list of short cuts
to avoid the BS

Walk woman walk
Like the beat in your heart is the one beneath your feet
When pressing soul tracks for the next generation
Never be afraid to rewind and refeet
Some songs you'll have to repeat
Your masters collection will be cool and complete
as long as you keep
walking
walk woman walk

PU GONG YING ON RENTON AVENUE

By Chris Clarke

The two women are small, earthen mounds

with white hats tied under their chins.

Their wrinkled hands grasp hammers

to pry the dandelions' roots

from the soil of Renton Avenue.

They have done this for years, for centuries

on the hardscrabble gravel of mountain ledges.

Their fingers, bone deep, extract medicine

from strata and sub-strata, to the heated core

where they pull life back from the edge.

They know the alchemists' mix of bitter herb

tempered with the cool elixir of love.

FREEDOM STILL ISN'T FREE

By Reagan Jackson

There is no breath in this body.

I have stretched to breaking

Everyday is more violent than the last

Another name,

Another crime,

Another hashtag,

Another story I'm ashamed to not want to remember

Where is my American amnesia when I need it the most?

Lost beneath the footage

Of another child shot and killed,

Another child thrown to the floor and beaten

Some mother's child

Turned victim

And there is no refuge from this violence,

No safe space to rest my eyes,

Closed eyes are for corpses.

The living, live to see, to witness

with bound hearts

the agony of cannon fodder

for a revolution

like the storm that never seems to break

that just looms promisingly

while the crops wither and die

leaving only strange fruits behind.

And they aren't confined to southern trees,

they fall from gunshots to northern knees.

They sprout up in the most unlikely places,

blossom on subway platforms or empty basins,

in locked jail cells strung up by their own laces.

The strange seeds have spread

Like pestilent weeds

And I can't breathe.

I can't

write another funeral poem

Can't create a sufficient picket sign

Can't rationalize

Can't debate

Can't stand still

Can't meditate

Can't pray when my church has been set on fire

Can't unbreak my heart

Can't allow media to sedate me.

But mostly I just can't

        FUCKING

          breathe.

This is my country

And I just can't leave.

Can't believe

Can't understand

The difference between white liberals

and the ku klux klan

when both are complicit

one apologetic and one dismissive
because all lives matter
its the highest truth of equality
that all lives matter
except the lives of people
who look like
me.

There is no breath in this body
I am stretched to breaking
Broken, haunted, a walking reminder
That for some of us
Freedom still isn't free.

THE NORTH STAR

By Bennett Taylor

Skin may re-generate,
Bones be replaced,
Eyes see through new lens,
Memory erase.

Hands may craft new uses,
Feet walk new tracks,
Lips speak new tongues,
Souls pilot new crafts.

Perhaps God has a pulse
That, like all else, expires.
Time itself may soon dissolve
In its own currents.

So a distant day of reckoning
Is no comfort to the suffering.
"Freedom is abstract" they say
But slavery is tangible.

The lash and club bore in so deep
They touched our children's flesh.
The world we see is haunted
By the souls of un-mourned dead.

The conquerors have become trapped
In their own simulations;
Buried all our souls within
The tomb of their inheritance.

We still have a guiding light
That is our long lost heritage
That still shines so bright within
We can't help but to follow it.

I trust where my people lead.
We stomp out an ancient beat
Hoping to match the rhythm
Of our ancestor's feet.

Suffer the fan

By Larry Crist

Returning from the Seahawk superbowl loss
The cold vacant streets fill with surly fans,
half way and fully drunk, with chicken wing
rings round their lips, stained fingers, pissed off,
abuzz over that same last sad minute seared into memory,
all asking the same question—Why'd he throw it?
When a three yard run would have won the game?
How different this town would be had that ball
not been intercepted. There was a minute to spare.
A minute when everyone screamed FUCK and
slammed fists on blameless armrests, upset drinks,
scared cats, hit walls, woke children, made the dog
cower and yelp with this human display of animal fury
What were they thinking? What possible rational
was at work and whose head would roll?
A superbowl loss is not the usual time for firings
but someone's head needed to be offed

And the soft rain illumined streets seemed dangerous
and would worsen, as all this disappointment
and anger fed toward the train stop, coalescing
into existential sorrow and multiplied rage
as train cars filled with blue and green jerseys, with
the names and numbers of these gladiatorial gods,
whose one careless play among all the others obliterated
happiness in this town. And the doors closed like razor

blades as the train moved south, and a fight nearly broke out
though most were sullen with exception to the random sob,
sudden curse or bitter chortle, listening to one angry young
man, wearing Marshawn Lynch's numbered jersey, vowing
aloud that he was going home and make himself a hotpocket
sandwich and drink a forty ouncer, and described the rest
of his sad angry night, and even the rest of his sad angry year
—a year only just begun—as ruined, until football season
reconvened; that he was mad and planned to stay that way
until the rains turned to sun and the sun learned to weep
and suffer as much as he

PERFECT WINE WASTED

By Isaac Robinson

I am like a perfect wine, nothing more.
Thick dark red, as blood.
I am drunk deeply, to the core.

Rare are the days I am enjoyed on the shore.
Yet, I am thrown away and stepped on as mud.
I am like a flawless white wine, nothing more.

My life is selfless, never a chore.
I am alone, unlike a flower bud.
I am drunk deeply, to the core.

Awful nights I am spit out, abruptly, a bore.
Hurt, lonely, and useless as a bomb dud.
I am a perfect wine, nothing more.

I am close to you, not vice versa, a closed door.
My emotions, abused, and used, a trapped flood.
I am drunk deeply, to the core.

The wine I am, useless today, thrown to the floor.
Wasted I lie down, defeated, free flowing blood.
I am like a perfect wine, nothing more.
I am drunk deeply to the core.

It's Happening Here, It's Happening There

By Jeanne Morel

We're part of the problem, my husband says when I complain. With a cord of charcoal I map the neighborhood from memory. Exhibit A: Among The Missing — the refugee office I worked for thirty years ago, Big John's Barber Shop, Rainier Office Supply. When Obama comes to visit, he will go to the library and talk about how his mother lived in a small house on Ferdinand, just one block south of me, and how his grandfather was in the furniture business before they moved to Hawaii. I'm not sure how to draw the time before Obama or I were born, or the waters of the Pacific Ocean, or a map of Hawaii, so I start to doodle instead. Grey lines and circles like my father used to draw on a small notepad when he talked on the telephone. Or rather listened — late into the night. I put down my charcoal to pose for a photo on a blue couch under a Japanese woodblock print in my living room — a woman holding a dead bird upside down while the cat, the husband, and the children look on. I stare into the eyes of the woman and she stares back at me. What's happening here happens all over the world. I chart a constellation of gold stars to illuminate the upscale restaurant strip that sits, a colonial crown upon the indigenous street. According to the *New York Times* reporter in Siem Reap, *Less than a decade ago there were no hotels with infinity pools, no restaurants serving fricassee of wild boar, no silk merchants who took VISA.* Rubbing my charcoal back and forth across the paper, I draw a curtain around the perimeter of the Darigold plant down the road, a relic from another era where I step over dead rats and breathe the stench of the sewer. The Chinese brothel with the acupressure charts in the window is closed, shut down by the cops. Last night I saw a police car pull up and park on the curb — blue lights over amber flashes. I crush the charcoal to capture lines and dashes, smudge the edge. My father liked early maps that weren't entirely accurate. There's more to truth than that. I walk to the kitchen. Like my father, I fry onion and garlic in olive oil every evening. Only later do I turn on the fan.

THE NORTH BEACON HILL CANTO

By Koon Woon

I will pay for the breeze, brief as it is,
rippling across the shroud of green leaves
over the ravine, on this sun brightened day,
in my Beacon Hill neighborhood,
where life is idle, and Dylan Thomas would pronounce it good.

On rainy days even, it boasts of a solitary café:
[The Station],
as in a station of the metro,
"the apparitions of these faces in a crowd"
(a small intimate crowd it is),
"petals on a wet, black, bough."

And would it have been worth it,
to order a tea, coffee, or cocoa,
marshmallow or orange marmalade
that will take you to another level of glad?
Like a walk from the house at a fresh hour of the morn,
inclined so slightly is 18th Avenue South,
spritely I jaunt past houses with eaves and green paint,
past shrubs manicured and the variegated roses that grace
communal pledges that we made
to rescue each from days that are sad,
as the gardens were mastered by gardeners
who measure without malice and weigh without hate.

Cross Beacon Hill Avenue with me to the Red Apple,
a house of plenty on this hilltop.
Take your sums from the Wells Fargo ATM,
go inside the store and give your eyes a feast,
and remember to purchase a book of stamps,
for letters to connect with Texas and Tennessee.
Let's now continue past the branch library,
but we will not linger now, for there is time,
time for you and time for me,
time for the hope of the woman,
even though the principle has been hijacked
by the congressional corporations.
O Ezra Pound, where are you now?
Thou were the CEO of Modernist Poetry.
Why did you take up residence at Saint Elizabeth?
Oh well we won't go see the Muse,
and even without a single glimpse of the Muse,
the walk must go on; we shall go on.

Inside his mind was the Muse.
And she moves on, as the river;
as the water, she moves on.
Stones will not impede her.
Shameless she provides,
in the estuary,
when birds rest from their flight.

That was another time.
He was on an island most of his days,
protected from unprivileged eyes.

She called for the sky,
there came the sky.
She wanted rain.
She became fertile again.

As I walk now past the bicycle shop
again on Beacon Hill Avenue,
I am of this place and of this time.
There is another coffee shop,
but I won't mention it by name when
the streets parade by with their designations
Horton and Hinds, Spokane at the Fire Station.
This is the loneliness of a long-distance intellectual,
the prelude with the pen that can enslave
better than an interminable sentence.

De la sierra, morena
Cielito lindo vienen bajando
Un par de ojitos negros
Cielito lindo de contrabando

Ay, ay, ay, ay, canta y no llores
Porque cantando se alegran
Cielito lindo los corazones

We do not object.
We do not object to its price.

Jin tien wo men cher fan
Wo men do shih cher fan

"In the café the women come and go,
Talking of Michaelangelo."

The Lotus Who Emerged From the Mud

by Darozyl S. Touch

To my dearest Love,

Has anyone ever told you,
You are a Lotus who emerged from the mud?
You rose from the depths of despair; of murky earth;
Of chains holding you hostage;
of burden on your shoulders;
pushing past the pain is like
pushing through boulders.
Slow death as your Father;
Stone cold as your Mother;
of silence as your shield;
of failure as your fear.
For all of these reasons,
you've shed your share of tears—
But Nothing, My Dear,
can change the conditions from which
you were born here.

So just STOP for a moment — and silence yourself.
Quiet your conscience and quit lying to yourself.
Give credit where credit is due — you have gone through so much pain
but the blame is not on you.
You can't control what other people do
so please don't give up;
You are made with resilience as a fighter — a true diamond in the rough
Recognize the intrinsic worth of your circumstance,

And thank the Creator for giving you this lifetime as a chance,

For you to blossom into the beautiful creation you were destined to be,

That even the sun would rejoice and sing,

"Oh, how you shine more radiantly than me!"

As you continue to grow, you will swiftly rise above,

The muck and the mire and all the earthy mud.

You will Rise up from what

entangled, entrenched, and bound you from the light,

That even your timeless beauty will captivate all in sight.

When your petals blossom to unveil your potential—

you will see,

Just how uniquely special you were created to be,

So you can truly appreciate

how your existence is extraordinary,

As a lotus undefined by your circumstance,

transcending adversity.

So, Awaken now, and bring your truth to light—

Victoriously unscathed,

you were and always have been,

created to fight;

By virtue of existence here on this earth,

You will inevitably endure pain and hurt.

But do remember, that your strength and power emanate from this earthen dirt.

So don't set limitations on yourself to rise above,

Because You are the Radiant Lotus who emerged from the mud.

REALITY CHECK

by Tymon Haskins

Che Taylor shot in the back

Seattle own son lost

Mike Browns body lay for hours with no care

TreVan Martin's hoodie couldn't cover his head from the cold of this world

Eric Gardner's knees slowly fell to the choking of the pain of historical and systemic racism

Jesus wept

His tears fell to the ground

His heart broken for the pain of this world

Tamir's innocence was taken before he got to the play the game of life

Sandra Bland's words were lost and confined by the jailhouse of slavery

Jesus listens

His heart is open

He longs to hear the cry

He fights to hear the mourning heart

He listens to the voiceless cry and wordless prayer

Unknown voice that was ignored when they called for help

Unfiltered anger when the door of opportunity is closed

Unrecognized pain when the world stabbed you in the back

Jesus speaks hope

Jesus holds tightly

Jesus speaks life

Jesus holds tightly

Your provide what I need

Reality check

Always available
Readily available
Always available
Readily available

Reality check

Tv is not always truth

Reality check

The pain is for a season

Reality check

I can still hope

Reality check

I am valuable; I matter

Reality check

Check my reality so I can see your reality

Reality check

LAMENT FOR A MOTH

by T. Clear

Lost, to a single point of electric light,
you surrendered to a false moon

in ever-diminishing circles,
spiraled to an end on a sidewalk

outside the Hummingbird Saloon.
And then trampled by someone's urgency

for Doritos. No dirge
to attend the last sputtering dust

from your two pairs of wings.
Not a bee or fly to hover vigil.

Never to know the straight line,
the perfect angle by which to navigate

along the horizon by moonlight,
by gene-encoded directionals

spun through egg, larva, pupa
for 190 million years. To end here,

swept aside in a twirl of wind,
more weightless than ever

minus your own spark of desire.
O my nocturnal, my less-than-lovely,

my little lepidopteron, where
will you not go now?

A Man in the Wind

by Gui Jean-Paul Chevalier

Who is in the wind,

A Man like sorrow, still, here stood.

In fight Deceived

No report

Beyond Desert Miles, Cities praise forgotten time,

sister to traveled memory

 From the road, Fragments like splinters of salty years dust trodden paths,

Between storms of blistered sand, The Story unfolds.

The cloths to shield the currier,

 protect yet filter smells of neighbor's taxed sins.

But the Man in the wind, listened to secret hand and plucked from beneath
hurried step.

He is every tale to feel,

let it be my story

Obscure is ever lonely as un-sifted truth.

Mourning Mornings

by TyCeleste

Mornings.

Filled with struggles, to get out of bed.

Filled with reasons, my heart bled.

Filled with pressure, for survival of the day.

Worries of where, my head will lay, approaching the sunset of today.

Filled with yesterday's lack of success, according to life's test.

Filled with the negativity, I fought so hard, to rid of by falling asleep.

Filled with the pressure, … I'm sinking in deep.

Filled with "I can't" and "I won't" to "I don't even know."

Filled with mother's and aunt's get up crow.

Filled with who, what,when, where, why and how?

How, did I find myself, in the morning.

How do I walk, talk, and smile, when all the while, … mornings.

Mornings pass, and days they do too.

Nights are not the only trouble it's true.

While some are resting, safe and sound

Others attempt to rest while holding a frown.

Grateful for the life we have left,

Life is truly the beginning, not a pass or fail test.

It's a journey to be seen.

To be heard.

To grow.

For the whole world to know.

I CAN

I can, make a difference in myself.

I can, make a difference in my family.

I can, make a difference in my community.

I can, make a difference in my nation.

I can, make a difference in the world.

I can, make a difference through hope, education, and action.

The Freedom School Story. Yet to know?

We believe in each other ... encourage each other to grow.

Our history pushes us through,

Holding on to what we know, to make our dreams come true.

Motivate instead of discriminate, we glow.

Recognizing each other, as we chant each other on.

Cheers for one another turn into song.

Announcing: No Child Will Be Left Behind.

We coerce,

Coerce the world to,

SEE | ME, My Life Matters.

No child poverty, no child delinquency.

We have already won.

This story continues,

Each day harambee begins.

Who's is the writer or is it already written?

DESPITE THE WAY IT HAS BEEN

Alvin "LA" Horn

You better stop

Smell the roses

Notice the plant life in the cracks of the sidewalk

Sip the coffee or juice of life

Bop you head to your music

The jam, the one song in the rhythm of your soul

Kick the volume up

Look in the windows as you pass-by

See your reflection and know there is nothing more beautiful

That image can't argue with you

You control any change, if that's what you want

You go in your own flow

Spend your dime

As you please

Live this life

Love your life

Always unveiling

Something new

Incorporating the old

Accepting everything must change

Yet you control the speed and the limit

So

Despite the way it has been

Make your reflection honor you and yours

You can keep on seeing the reflection in the window as you pass-by and
know there is nothing more beautiful

After Several Sharp Caws in Succession

By Martha Silano

Something about orcas not having a complex language.
Something about a scale, human language at the top.

Something if they're so smart why don't they skip
the King, pig out on ubiquitous Coho and chum.

Something about picking blackberries without Galway Kinnell,
his *stalks very prickly*, a line I've been repeating since 1984.

Something about C02, each year seven million more metric tons.
Something called the Alberta Tar Sands, where 50,000 acres

of goopy black bitumen become two million barrels a day,
Soon they will double production. Soon the tankers will cruise

through the Salish Sea, where the orcas spend half the year.
Something about a Goldilocks planet circling its sun

the same distance as Earth orbits hers, only this planet's
1,400 light years away. Only this planet could be gaseous.

Those, if there, if alive, dutifully drilling in their equivalent
of the Arctic, marveling at the rapid melting of permafrost.

(Something about irony. Something about imagination).
Something about not knowing, as in Kinnell's poem,

the thing *unbidden*, like *one-syllabled lumps*, like *toad*,
like *moth*, like *life as we knew it*. Something about

acceleration, a measurement called the albedo, percentage
of light absorbed by the Earth: none, a little, a lot. So many

somethings, unfrozen or charred, emitting methane
and carbon—trees and grass turned against us.

Snow repels light; the widening oceans absorb it exponentially
(is that what he said?). *Locked in a post-glacial warming trend,*

said the woman who said she'd pick up my daughter, running late,
having already been across town and back before the sun rose over

the Cascade crest. Can't pick berries, not think of *squinched,*
same sharp pain as the girl in New Jersey I was, same leaning in.

Something about the bees not seeming to mind a lack
of discernible breeze, grass the color of sand, no trace

of green. Not late September but early August, the news
not icy but the warmest summer on record; we've surpassed

1958. He said he splurged well but when asked said he wasn't
a nature poet. Humans, he said, have taken over, have disregarded

numbers like 1.7 billion, age of the oldest of Death Valley's rocks,
forgotten the cultural lives of crows. Something about the ice

not caring. The sun. How the parts per million of carbon
don't give a damn; they just keep going up.

A Doll Like Me

By Kiana Davis

I cried for dolls
that didn't always exist on shelves
shelves that held rows and rows of dolls
for a little girl I did not know

when I got older
and stopped insisting
that all brown dolls
looked like me
stopped begging
my mother for an image
of myself to hold

she told me
she had been afraid
to come home from shopping
empty handed
afraid to bring her little girl
a pink, blue eyed, stranger

she blamed Reagan
for their absence
convinced that before him
she had no problems
finding brown dolls
for her daughters

she told me
that sales clerks stared at her
not understanding why
she couldn't take any doll from their shelves
she said she searched stores
close to tears for me.

all I remember of those times is:
crying because I didn't understand the absence
crying because I had to leave stores empty handed
crying for a doll brown like me
crying because of pain I could not articulate

WHEN

By Alesia Cannady

When the clouds move, where do they go?

Gliding across the sky to and fro.

When the rain falls where does it land?

On a soft tongue or an open hand?

When the snow falls, Why is it cold?

To remind us of the young and the old.

When I whisper your name, what do you hear?

I love you my child have no fear.

WHY

By Lola E Peters

She wants to stand before him naked
Devoid of the burdensome mantle of history
Breasts unfettered by the requirements of others' needs
Belly free to breathe life deep
Womb available to pleasure

She leans her head toward his bare shoulder
And meets only the ends of barbs
Constructed to preserve his survival
Her mere touch opening near-healed wounds
His recoil her ever-present rejection

She stands before him fully costumed
Each layer self-reinforced
Stanching pain at its root
He sees untouchable mystery
She sees unreachable strength

Together they die alone.

What If

by Tiffani Jones

What if the world went on for infinity?

Would good and bad things never have an ending?

If so, would racism, sexism, and terrorism go on?

And only some people be peaceful, loving and have fun?

What if the world had no wars, but peace?

And the number of kids in school only increased?

What if the world's people didn't wear make-up that hid them?

But knew they were as beautiful as the brightest gem?

What if the world could see everything through?

And only cared about the true you?

What if the world had only baptism and optimism?

That deleted all our pessimism?

What if the world was filled with love?

What if the world had all of the above?

Cookies and Water

By Kayla Blau

"Cookies and water" was written with chalk on the side of the shelter today

The kids set up a lemonade stand-esque business model

Bought corner store cookies with couch cushion coins

Flipped off brand Oreos at 300%

Chilled the water jug in the freezer like the young entrepreneurs they are

Mom's EBT card got lost in the mail again

This is dinner

This is taking malleable minds off emptiness

Off Hot Cheetos for breakfast

Off no one coming home

Off no home to come home to

"Cookies and water"

"We made $22.47 today!!"

Such pride in their pockets

This filling holes

This ends unmet

For what it's worth

They've learned no one hears you

with that many

Holes in your pockets

The Living Of It

by Christy Karefa-Johnson

There was the night I stood battered
and so infused with God
at my mother's door
with no flowers,
worming towards the cracks in her structure
with the marrow of a fallen angel
smeared between the knuckles.

There we watched the daytime sputter
and spit loose molars of white light to the sky.
We've heard, though no one's ever told us,
that in the levitating folds
of each evening's pink exodus
a messiah is returning every second.

There is something that knows the Earth as an ant

Maybe the manatee that tries to swim
and just gets cut.

AHYH

by Dustin Washington

I float in my created womb of silence
Seeking answers undefined from minds un-evolved
I've been alone for so long
But still disconnected from my first soul
I am imperfect but divine

A meteor of fire through space and time
On an endless quest for truth
I am power restrained
Seeking to bloom
I am the wars to be and the wars of past
Nothing escapes my grasp

I hold the shadow in hands of patience
Illuminating darkness with the stars in my eyes
I have begun the final journey to forever
Stare into the night sky and watch me rise

BIKING TO THE P-I

by Kristen Millares Young

I

Biking up Beacon Hill never makes you feel good. First there's the right turn up Alaska, waiting at the MLK intersection for the light to change, and then it's time to pop up in the pedals and give it all you've got, which isn't much by the time you hit the incline on the other side of the boulevard. Here, the road begins its ascent, and you're peddling, and for a while, you think, I've got this, I've totally got this, but you're slowing, still standing in the pedals, and now you're downshifting, and the blackberry bushes aren't flashing by anymore. You can see their thorns and the matted trails made by the homeless, and you're in first gear, nowhere to go but up. You're going, but now you taste the diesel, and the sidewalk's gone to shit, and that family left their recycling bin in their driveway again, and one weave is enough to make you wobble so you're sitting, sucking wind and fumes and hawking loogies at the top of the hill, where everyone looks at you, shaking their heads, glad to be in their cars. Stupid white girl.

II

I'm Cuban, B!

III

Cresting Beacon Hill is just the beginning, because this was before the mayoral campaign about bike trails, and the only paint on the street marks the potholes. You try not to notice how close the cars come, and you're focusing on the golf course with the small stooped men lugging their clubs, and by this time your clothes are clinging, and it's no good to pretend that half of that isn't sweat, which is the great fallacy of wearing rain gear to exercise. Your jacket opens when you lean over to change gears, and you can smell yourself, glad there's a shower at the newsroom where you won't have a job much longer. But you don't know that now, so as the Escalades roll past, trailing bass and blunt smoke, you inhale, hoping to get high so the deadlines won't make you sick to your stomach again. When you get to the intersection at 12th, you hop onto the sidewalk to beat the light, and soon you're back on the road, flying past parked cars — please don't open your door, please don't open your door, please don't open your door — you want to live though it's raining and you're screaming down to the 12th Avenue bridge, and then there's Smith Tower and the Sound. Seattle shows you what she's got through the mist and rain, and you're glad to be alive though it's wet and cold and you're only halfway there.

IV

The thing about stereotypes is that sometimes they're true, and that's part of what makes them infuriating to everyone involved. You take a left on Jackson because though the bike map says Dearborn you know that isn't the best way. Here, stop signs are suggestions, and some people drive like every time is the first time. So you take Jackson, and that means carts full of oranges, that means carts full of fish, that means buses and buses, and then that lady is riding your ass like she wants to touch it, her bumper so close you can feel the heat of her engine, and when you finally get to the light, you do it, you give her the finger and scream stay off my ass, and for the next six blocks, she's wagging her finger at you because you just disrespected an elder. Your abuela would be ashamed. For the rest of your ride, you smile and nod at everyone you see, so they'll feel acknowledged and you can stop feeling like you killed something small.

V

The Alaskan Way Viaduct is dangerous, everybody knows it, the next time the ground shakes it'll smack flat as a pancake but the oozing berries will be cars. Beneath it's dark even in full daylight, and it smells like rape, and you know that's what happens here because you've heard it before, because you'll hear it in ten minutes, where's the rape story? shouted from the breaking news editor, and the retort, open your eyes, RAPE16 is in already, and the bitterness of trading trauma this way will grind you down until you decide to wear earplugs that blacken with time. But for now, you're cruising along the bike lane, and you have to remember to slow down at the intersections because that's where they'll get you. You emerge at the port and hope those people don't see you because they started hating you after the federal investigation, and you don't know how to tell them anything but, this is my job, to expose your incompetence and corruption, but not until after coffee and a shower.

I Saw You This Morning

by Alvin "LA" Horn

I saw you this morning

I saw you at the bus stop

I saw you driving the opposite way with the convertible top down

I saw you walking in the store

Then I saw you walking out the store

I saw a coffee in your hand and you were smiling

I saw you reading a book by Alvin L. A. Horn at a park while sitting on a bench

I saw you laying on a blanket at the beach sunning yourself

I saw you coming down the stairs as I was headed up

I saw you going in that building and I wondered did you see me as I passed you

Wherever I see you, I swear you must be the most beautiful woman I've ever seen

Although you're not just one, you are all

In all your comings and goings you are all the women of the world

God's gift to the world and man

Today you are the most beautiful, but then aren't you always... I think so

I saw you in every shape and form

You are tall ...you are short ...you are athletic ...you are thin ...you are curvy...you are sexy...

You were in the color of coffee and coffee and cream ...you were in the color of blackberry... you were in the color of brown sugar and redbone you were the colors that allowed me to see your freckles ...you were the color of lemon meringue pie ...you are the color of banana pudding ...you were all the colors in the sky

You were that color of that color crayon that nobody can seem to remember the name of that color

You were in the color of soul...

You were in the color of love

I saw you this morning I wondered did you see me

I wonder... will there be one-day, you see me as I'm passing by

As I'm driving by with my top down

As I'm walking in the door

As I'm walking down the street

At the train station

Coming off the plane or boarding and I'm sitting across from you...will you see me

Might you be there at the end of my journey waiting for me

All I do know for sure is...

I saw you today and you are absolutely beautiful, and you are everytime I see you

I'm behind you wishing you'll turn around and see me

THE NUMBER 7: GOT CHANGE?

by Nikkita Oliver

There are things about this city
only the buses know
For the most part they keep her secrets
But the 7 has blown past me
Whispers of past relationships
At first sight lovers that do not exist anymore
Places dined in by only the most seasoned of Seattleites

Her favorite spots are becoming ghosts
Holes in her stockings
Soon only the buses will blow through

Lately she's been getting all dolled up for new guests
They do not know who she's been
Just who they want her to be

The 7 has seen the way she turns
Wraps herself 'round mountain and river
Bends her back over places we used to go
The Silver Fork that garnished her table is stolen
The 7 can't get full anymore

Rainier Avenue is not the partner she once was
Things are changing
Rapidly riding these new leaf blown opportunities
In the street the smell is getting stronger
Just caught a wiff of another lost prophet

In this place our rubber does not meet the road like it used to
The 7 used to know the children of the children
Till the babies started being pushed out
Farther souf', they can't catch up like they used to
So used to being used Seattle does not question her lost innocents

The 7 knows all the casualties
Knows how the route might look the same on paper
but so much has changed

Downtown whistles at buses
stuffed full of suits wearing capitalist dreams
Passerbys, they can't ID Mount Baker
and Seattle is not the climb she once was

The 7 tells Seattle to slow down
Columbia City is changing speeds
But she keeps spinning her wheels
Tugging at heartstrings
Trying to figure out what happened from
Hillman City to Rainier Beach

Missing the days of riding in packs
How the 7s never come
when they say
But roll by all at once
Just to show you
how many of them there are

Rarely on time
but always something
rare to find when you catch them

The 7 tells Seattle
"Beware,
How you're changing lanes
Cause we just aren't the same
anymore."

Seattle starts to cry
Like she always does
But somehow different

Remembers being told
Change is constant
And God is change

So the 7 remains holy—
Carrying the City's confessions
farther south
Out farther and farther away
from the city

PASSENGER

By Bennett Taylor

Last night I cruised around Saturn again.
Smoke and mirrors slowed light
Enough that I could catch it.
In the haze I felt your presence.
Sharp and vivid, without image.
I spoke to silence and it listened
But unasked questions go unanswered.

The world is ageless and distance nonexistent
From the driver's seat of a vehicle without destination.
I revisit our few memories in endless new places.
Yesterday: A Blockbuster video in Haiti.

This travel diary grows with every imagined route.
Fueled by delusion I get more miles to the gallon.
If we both believed in fiction, we could go any direction.
North, South, East, West, maybe even Forward and Back.

Dreams mean nothing in retrospect
Unless they drive the will to act.
The myth that love could transcend time
Sent me flying toward the sunset.

Now, with words, I build new wings.
Like sand, they crumble in my hands.
In patience, or madness
I'll gather what's left.

With improved design
I'll build them from scratch.
Tomorrow I won't be travelling alone.
Your echo is better than no you at all.
When I crack these windows, out you will go
And I'll drive this old car
Somewhere new.

AMERICAN CROSSING GUARD
RAINIER AVENUE SOUTH, SEATTLE

By Steve Potter

Omar at the halal deli
tells me of Ramadan,
fasting, the pilgrimage to Mecca
as he prepares my samosas to go.
He talks of his respect for Jews
and respect Jews have for Muslims.
Halal is kosher and kosher is halal.
He eats at the kosher deli
and Jews eat at the halal deli
because at both the meat is clean.
The animals are raised with respect
and they are butchered with respect
a fact I too, Pantheist
with Protestant roots, appreciate.

I walk out onto the avenue
past the Tobya Gallery of African Art.
A big group of kids from Franklin High
crosses at the corner.
They are all the same race
human
displaying the full range of complexions
the various branches
of our vast extended family
took on since we wandered away

from the Serengeti Plain
across Africa, Asia,
Europe and the Americas.

Farther south down the avenue
a gray-haired black man
in a blaze orange vest
smiles, nods and says, "hello."
He raises his whistle to his lips
and blares three sharp toots
while stepping into the crosswalk
raising his small red stop sign
halting the cars, ensuring the safety
of a group of grammar school kids
little sisters and brothers perhaps
of the Franklin High kids from before.
I would trade a million arrogant,
hateful American snipers
for this one humble, caring
American crossing guard.

We are making something happen here
all of us now together,
despite institutional racism
despite religious intolerance

despite white supremacy
despite ethnocentrism
despite lingering distrust
from centuries of cruelty,
we are making something happen here
all of us now
together.

I Tell You, Italio

By Seth Paradox

The birds are the future
Our youngest order
Evolution's children

The sea within us is vast
Swept with tides
Towards the future

Flight and flowing
From the ocean to the air
We go, are going, eternally drawing near

Boldly, we scrape the blue of heaven
With our swift wings
Our future beings

SPARROW AND DOVE

by Syd Denise Fredrickson

A Sparrow and a Dove sat and talked to one another.
Long ago, far away, each was intrigued by the other.

Sparrow chirped, while Dove would coo
And their conversation flowed.

Like a song it warbled on
A pleasant harmony they sowed.

Then the Raven with its beak came and broke into their song.
"Don't you know," he said to them, "this mixing of the flocks is wrong?"

"No," they said, and turned away.
"We do not like the rules you give."

So they sang to one another,
And more happily they lived.

ORCA FIN

By Minnie A. Collins

If I could listen to rumbling timber mills, cracking and whacking of
falling trees,

If I could smell smoldering firecracker factories,

If I could imagine streams meandering down to lakes, rivers, flowing
into the bay, the sound, the ocean,

If I could track Duwamish and Costal Salish foot trails to winter cedar
long house camps, nestled among fir and hemlock,

If I could fish, hunt, heed elders' oral histories or remember bear
sighting tales,

I can imagine how myriad moons ago

Orca, steering through streams, currents, crossing inlets, breaching

Driven by keel-like fins, became caravans of seafarers charting their course

And remembering currents.

Orca fin now forged in Columbia City; now cast in bronze, copper, glass

Revive forgotten, foggy meandering streams and coastal foot trails

Where concrete blue tiles mark yet mock Salish Spirits;

Upright Orca fin, translucent and orbital

Reflects past and present town life.

Once fireworks factory jobs, now fireworks, parades, and dragon whirligigs

Once timber mill jobs, now manmade fiber boards and no jobs

Once indigenous people, now cultural convergence, in cordial yet wavering
currents,

History

By Georgia S. McDade

"The Sixties people dropped the ball!
They let us down, left us hanging!"

It took everything to cover what could have
      been a "Go, Hawks" scream.
How could she say that?

Not wanting to hurt or condemn, I sat fuming
as the conversation moved to other topics.

The comment made me answer how we did
    not drop the ball, how we carried, carry
    the burden today, how scars cover our
    bodies mentally and spiritually and
    sometimes physically.
We went to all of those white high schools
    and colleges where so many people did
    not want us to go. We usually skip
reunions.
The fun part of these educational institutions
    never materialized for us: we spent most
    of our time alone or in a corner with the
    one or two other black students; people
    shut doors in our faces; they bumped into
    us; they knocked books out of our hands.
    Teachers were rarely helpful. If the
    principal was involved, we were almost
    always the ones suspended or expelled.

Many of us had to go to another school or
university; some of us never completed formal school.
On the rare occasions when a white student
asked us for help with an assignment, that student
 got a B and we got a D.
We were told we should be in another department.
We were encouraged to change our majors.
We were encouraged to take sabbaticals — all
      we had to do was write the dissertation.
Upon attempting to re-enter, we were told we
      did not meet the requirements. One man
reluctantly took a sabbatical at his advisors'
suggestion—allow others to participate in
this small program, advisors said. When he
attempted to re-enter, he was told his 3.8 grade
point was too low. The program required a 3.5;
"We have so many applicants with 4.0 that we
are not looking at anything but 4.0 grade points."
After years of attempting to get terminal
degrees, we received letters, letters
telling us the school had made an error,
we should not have been admitted to the
program.
Some of us left one university and went to
      another where we discovered what we
      had left.

Some of us went to other countries; one

    friend went to Scotland, got his Ph. D.

    too.

We endured parents who said, "Leave those

white people alone. When the Lord is

ready for you to go in those places, He'll

make a way."

And some of us went to jobs where we found

    ourselves in the same situation. Despite

    how good we were, we were always

"affirmative action" employees and definitely not qualified. We were the
    token one or one of two or three. We trained persons who were younger, less

    educated, less experienced, and less

skilled. These trainees were often

promoted to jobs we never got.

Because of our singlemindedness, some of us are

poor spouses and poor parents. Because of our preoccupation, we divorced or
    were divorced, some of us more than once.

Some of us are mentally and spiritually and
    often physically scarred. Half a century later we continue to ask ourselves did
    we do what needed to be done. We want to know if we had taken another route
    if all would be better now. We can't stop thinking about that time.

Whether we got the degrees or not, we paid a

high price, younger sister. Those of us still here are still paying. Drugs, alcohol,
    prison, suicide took some of us. So much

of what you can do today is the result of standing on our

shoulders, shoulders that are often invisible to you.

How different would life be if we had chosen to sit

through the Sixties?

There are more examples. These were the first to come to mind.

All of a sudden I thought about how long I was upset with Roy Wilkins.

I kept telling myself that he should have

known better. He was an adult; we were

kids. What did we know?

Then one day as clearly as could be I realized

that Roy Wilkins was not guilty. He was almost as innocent as we were
Roy Wilkins had no way of knowing just how much of a battle integration
would be. He could never have imagined that some human beings would
treat other human beings in such a sub-human fashion. Perhaps he had
never thought legislatures can never legislate what transpires in hearts and
minds. I immediately forgave him, wish I could have thanked him.

So, I realize the young lady did to us Sixties

     folks what I did to Mr. Wilkins.

Perhaps one day she will see as I see.

How many times do we have to take the same hills?

As many times as we have to take the same hills.

Some hills can't be given to the enemy.

AND we have to hear that others view our

accomplishments as nil or near nil.

Dear younger brothers and sisters, though we lost thousands, maybe
millions with the assassinations of Dr. Martin Luther King, Jr., and Senator
Robert F. Kennedy, the great majority of us are still here, still fighting.

Many of us continue working never having gotten the justice at the end
of that arc. We take care of children and grandchildren, neighbor
children, go to school meetings, teach—often without pay. Despite
being in our sixties, seventies, eighties, and even nineties, many
of us continue to carry the ball, we have never dropped it.
We did not leave you hanging.
We never would.

SO MANY SOULS. SOME LOST, SOME FINDING THEMSELVES, OTHERS UNAWARE OF THEIR OWN EXISTENCE

By Laurent B. Chevalier

This is a machine that both consumes and creates, utilizing the same raw matter of human capital. After a time, we are all to some degree both product and prey. Some fall prey to a greater degree, being selected a victim to be trampled underfoot. Others still, draw a golden ticket, plucked from the masses of their peers, and elevated to heights unfathomable in any other location.

Full of terrible beauty, the skyscrapers earn their name, grating against the blue up above as if finger nails reaching for the last crumbs. And below, there is a mass, providing foundations from which the buildings rise.

It is in that mass that the identity is found. The old, the young, the rich, the poor and literally everything in between. Here, bodegas sell cans of King Cobra around the corner from Imams facing east. Here, eyes that have seen world wars wait for trains underground, moving from home to store to home, alone. Here, everyone is a Columbus, traveling 30 minutes to discover new worlds. Here, sweet summer nights are at the same time unbearable and cherished. Cursed for the enveloping heat, wept for when they are exchanged for the icy darkness.

All those here seek to find their wings, stretching out to expand their personal horizons. New York is the flame to fly to, the determination of whether you're a moth or a Phoenix. These are the New Yorkers.

DUCK AND COVER

by Robert Zverina

In a black-and-white photo from the 1950s,
kindergarteners are crowded into a corner,
bent over Indian-style, shirts ride up
bony backs exposed to the imminent threat.

Teacher, corsage erupting at her breast, looms
over fingers locked to protect vulnerable necks,
points and implores — *Kiss the floor!* — and the children
double in fear, tremble and strain all the more.

An air raid siren rattles the windows somewhere
beyond the photograph's border, its warning ignored
by the impassive camera whose blinding white bulb
blooms in a petaled reflector. Conditioned to cower,
they try for their knees, what they're told is safety.

All except the one Colored girl who stares without fear
into the flash. Having lived her whole life at ground zero,
she alone accuses and has nothing to lose.

Online Dating

By Emily Williamson

Agnostic, libertarian, anarchist
Decline, dismiss, reject
We write each other off
With a single click.

You don't like his freckles
Not a fan of his brow
His nose is too crooked
Smile looks like a scowl

That same guy you meet
Might sweep you off your feet
Whisk you away
On a romantic vacay

She doesn't want to be a mom
She's divorced
And that seems wrong
You pass her over
Onto the next
Certain to find
The very best!

If you met her at a party
Got to know her at your friend's
You might feel your heart flutter
You might ask to be her man

We are so much more than labels
Than selective profile photos
Each unique individuals
Dig down deeper
Those dislikes might be fables

Hear their story
Touch their soul
Watch their personality shine
When they talk about life's goals

No longer a stranger
They've become your friend
Someone who'll stick with you
To the very end.

Unsolicited Advice for a Black Girl too Light to be Heavy but too Heavy to be White

By Nikkita Oliver

When the girl in your class fixes her lips
to call your mother a "nigger lover"
Fix her face
So next time she thinks twice
Before fixin' her lips around anyone's mama

When the kids on the playground start to sing
"Jungle Fever"
Join them
You must live
to fight another day

When the school principal calls
you into her office
to account for it all
Tell her to call yo' Mama

When your white Mama
does not answer
the way you need her
Know that it is ok to be angry
She will never understand
what it is to be brown
She will come to see
white and light
are not the same thing

When proper speech becomes an allegation

code switching an accusation

When sounding white and acting black

become corners in your mouth

you cannot fight

Bring them together

like puckered lips

give your self a kiss

In you these things

are not in opposition

they are one

in the same

Beautiful

When your hair becomes fighting words

Your off-beat claps an inside joke

Learn how to tie your hair up quick (so it does not get pulled)

Learn to laugh (at yourself)

Get in the mirror,

Learn how to furrow your brow,

how to ball up your fist,

Learn how to show them

your serious face

Also, buy a Walkman,

seriously

Make mix tapes off the radio,
practice your tootsie roll,
butterfly,
cabbage patch,
harlem shake
until you have perfected their rhythm
for public exposure and
middle school dances

Take walks with your Walkman,
snap, clap, dance to your hearts content
Therein lays the only beat that truly matters
You are only off-beat with your self
when you are not true to your self
So be true baby girl
And remember what your Mama always says:
At least you can sing

When your black grandmother calls you white
cause you don't like grits
When your white grandmother calls you black
cause you ate all the greens
Don't eat the grits
Eat the greens
Or eat the grits
Don't touch the greens

If you are gonna be what you eat
then be exactly who you want to be

When the white boys do not want to date you
When the black boys do not want to date you
When the black girls and the white girls
do not want to be your friend

because they think all of the boys want to date you,
say:
Fuck 'em
Cause the first man to kiss you will be Samoan
The first women will be racially ambiguous

It is ok to see the gaps in human thinking
and wonder why we live these boxes
When your box becomes too small
Get out!
Do not live a slow death
Boxes come soon enough for us all

When you realize that something has come
and infected us all
When you cannot find the right words
to explain it
Do not blame yourself
Do not carve indictments into your own skin

The world will do enough
to put your flesh on trial

Do not feel guilty
For acknowledging the ways that we,
humans, hang our skin on dry bones
Building tents
where there are already holy temples

You mixed black girl
be beautiful holy temple
When too light to be heavy
When to heavy to be white
Be black light exposure
For you own zebra stripes
Never half of anything
Always everything holy you

So that when the girl at school fixes her lips
To call your mama a "nigger lover"
You can ball up your fist,
furrow your brow,
let out a laugh, and
Show her
How seriously you love

On a Young Man Writing at King County Juvenile Detention Center

By M.S. Johnson

A kid in juvie knows
old and dead are not the same—
old is not dead yet;

what it's like to live
amid an upturned orchard,
broken limbs, torn roots,

rampant bulldozers
having plowed his homeland under
as no righteous god would ask,

his mother lost,
needle in a burn pile,
his leg, bullet-grazed;

knows enough to feel
gangbanging's gotten old,
knows it's not yet dead,

but not how to start
an orchard,how scion joins
rootstock, what graft works best,

just that he needs to;
which neighbor to ask — someone,
he knows, he must trust.

It may or may not
be someone he knew, even
the same god, or me,

the neighbor who knows
nothing but orchards, not god,
not what needs writing,

that he's counting on
to tell him why he's here, why
choose old over dead,

help him find live words
to describe the death he left,
knows needs outliving.

That he sees his word
matters, splices in a bud,
pits hope against long odds:

odds I long will yield.

I am From...

By drea chicas

This is where I am from

I am from you have an accent, you're not from here, so we went back to our country

I am from coffee farms in El Salvador as far as your eyes can see

I am from sopa de gallina

Break that chicken's neck, because we're hungry

I am from rivers de agua viva, give us back its waters, because we're thirsty

I am from callused hands picking lettuce and fruit of our best harvest

They stole our land, so we fought back

I am from cumbias frescas sazonadas with gospel and live jazz

I am from no tenes pelos en la lengua

"Razor edges on her tongue" (LHL)

I am from red, white, and blue, ella la Americana

Blue with melancholy, mourning murdered sons on red stained pavement

I am from libraries of indigenous and african warriors, story-telling your future

I am from a highly educated Mami of a bended knee theology

I am the curious seed of a learner, Papi's boxing legacy

I am from a healing people, the Great Physician has come for us

Carrying tamales and pupusas de queso

I am from children chanting in the streets, Freedom, Freedom we want freedom, AND we hear them, that is where I am from

ACT THREE

By Jaime Rodriguez

A safe haven

you were

a place to rest

my troubled soul

my aches and pains

a place to stay

as hours turn to days

hours to days

the time has come

for final bows

as curtain call descends

on this here play

in this moment

I bid farewell

adieu, adieu

The Roar of Remembrance (Rose)

By Marcus Harrison Green

There are times I cry out

To not see your face

or hear your voice

or sense your touch

But to remember

to remember…

Vagabond

By Jaime Rodriguez

I am the wanderer

the nomad

a drift from Mountain to Valley

and back again

no place to call home

The world is my home, my oyster

its peaks, valleys, rivers, oceans, forest all my home

I drift upon the sea of life

like driftwood

I am the remains of something ancient, long ago forgotten

I am the fossilized remains of the ancient dinosaur

who once proudly roamed the earth

I am now fodder for the hungry

shelter for the lowly

I am the foundation of something great yet to come

My Daughter's Eyes

By Monique Franklin

My daughter has the most beautiful eyes

she has the prettiest chocolate brown eyes

I have ever seen

when I see her eyes

I want to eat them all up

and when I eat them all up

Delicioso

those dark chocolate centers

see through to the center of my soul

and just take my love straight from the source

in those eyes

burns fire enough

to burn this whole place down

so the earth may be reseeded

growing the greenest lush ever imagined

in her eyes

in those eyes

there are questions that I am not ready with answers

they question you

they question me

it hurts to see

that her questions are already questioning she

I see pain

in my daughters eyes

in those eyes

is a fierce agent

equipped with intelligence and reason

sonic hearing devices that make we wish I didn't talk so

loud sometimes

with a memory to argue reality down to the seconds

creativity to trick the truth

she's definitely got her mother eyes

in her eyes

in those eyes

in my daughters eyes

the prettiest eyes

the fiercest eyes

the wisest eyes

I find joy

and when those sleepy eyes close

safely after another day of living

I find peace in her eyes

laying with my daughter in bed

last night

she started talking to me

in her poets voice

and she said:

"My mom has the most beautiful eyes

she has the prettiest chocolate brown eyes

I want to eat them all up

and when I eat them all up

I have ever seen

when I see her eyes

I say

Delicioso"

Boxing is Like Jazz

By Laura Wright

Boxing is like jazz

Like the break in the song when improvisation and creativity takes over

Like the challenging of seemingly fixed relations and patterns

Boxing is like jazz

It is knowledge and movement in all directions

Dissonant and yet resonant

It is grace and skill under intense pressure of held breath and notes
yearning to be released

Boxing is like jazz

It is the picking and choosing of the identity you will own in that moment

It is a movement that is too visceral for words

Giving us confidence to cope with any situation

Boxing is like jazz.

THE ECSTASY OF NOW

By Sampson Moore

there's a glint from a grim corpse you can see as it slithers from the dark grave

in dire search to reprise a role played so long ago that yesterday forgets

its head ascends in silence to glimpse a life it longed to live

if only it owned the courage it had to borrow

if only it possessed the passion it desired to lend

to view a vantage of life it housed in wishes and journeyed to in dreams

its bitter poison willfully swallowed now exchanged for the savory saccharine

and what was long exhaled is breathed in

the dead, the gone, mine ancient carrion so bewildered, can only peer at
future yesterdays

to see me smile wide enough to stretch the boundaries of a lifetime, from
what was, to what will be, all with the gleam from the exquisite today

On Aging

by Lola E Peters

All my grapes have turned to raisins
All my plums are shriveled prunes
A four-lane highway lines my forehead
Bumps and pocks turn me to ruins

It's not death that I find daunting
Not the end that looms ahead
It's this daily dehydration
Sagging face and arms I dread

They don't tell you when you're thirty
As heads turn when you arrive
It won't matter when you're sixty
Some things you just can't revive

The beauty and the ugly girl
Will wake up to betrayal
The genius and the brainless twit
Will have their projects fail

So glad I didn't hesitate
To do what gave me joy
But now comes the adjustment
Like that gorgeous gift from Troy

I'm not the grand dame some envision
I'm not the vixen I still see
One of these days I'll figure out
Who I'm now going to be

But in the here and now time
I'll do all that I can
To be the woman I enjoy
While I carve out a plan.

Not the end.

You are Loved

by Mahogany Cherrelle

If I had a loud speaker I would tell you you are loved and your value was never
meant to be found in a verdict anyway

Don't assess your worth based on others' hate

My brother, stand tall because you are a child of the greatest of all

The Father of lights so don't be blinded by the darkness

Consumed by rage and shame

Anoint yourself with oil daily and brother, gird your waist

You are brilliant, compassionate, and possess wisdom beyond your days

You are unshakeable, irreplaceable, and beautiful and unbreakable

Made in the image of God woman came from you and child from her womb

You see it all started with you, brother know your roots

It's only fitting that it end the same so stand up and take your place

At the head never the tail

At the top, never the bottom

Not to be forgotten because you are the apple of His eye

The Word says, blessed are the poor and blessed are those who mourn

So don't be surprised, brother, that your crown comes with thorns

LESS OF ME (MY BODY)

by Reagan Jackson

Touch me gently with voice and eyes
and hands that long to learn me
Tell me that if I become more than who I am now
your love will grow to match
that your heart is made of something
akin to stretch denim
large enough to hold these hips and thighs
make me believe it.

There should be less of me.
That has been the general consensus
of medical professionals, well intentioned gym teachers,
and kids on the playground
since I was 7 and baby fat became just fat.
Treadmills and lion tamers,
Weight Watchers and food journals
all failed to take this body
and make it into a suitable after picture.

Run little girl, run faster.
If you can't run the mile in under 12 minutes
how can you ever expect to outrun
the un-love that is coming for you
the teenage insecurities that will wrestle you to the ground
the parade of men who will tell you
you're simply too much woman.

Where will you find solace
when skinny blonds
wield their mirrors like knives
from the tops of every billboard
and no one notices
when you start to bleed.
No one notices…

There is something wrong
when loving your body as it is becomes
an act of political subversion.
I would love her anyway
wrap her in silks,
paint her in glitter and shimmy,
this reflection cast in the mold
of every woman I had ever loved
but I would do it knowing
I wasn't supposed to.

Keep nothing of this place,
they whispered.
And in those dreams
my other mothers would come to me
touch me gently with voices and eyes
Spirit hands soothing the love back into me
rocking me in their laps

even when I was grown
reminding me that I could
never grow too big to be held by God.

Keep nothing of this place,
they knit their prayers around me through the nights,
but in the harsh light of day
I would awaken to this impossibility.
How I can unsew the shadow
clinging to my heels?
Shed the very air around me?
We were born into one another
my America
and the body of my circumstances

This body is my anchor
my declaration that moving me will be difficult
that I can sustain myself
for a season of lack
that I am prepared to never have enough
of what I need to sustain myself
This body is my airplane crash survival kit.
The granite beneath the ideals
graffitied across my mirror,
the mountain that shrinks for no one.

There should be less of me,
and what is left should be lighter skinned
in skinny jeans with long blond hair
because barbies come in black now
and Beyoncé is beautiful.
The height weight index was not the first
to measure me
to quantify the exact percentage
of how much of me was too much
to be allowable.

I wake up wondering
when the anger won't awaken with me,
but I could no sooner
peel the nerves from my skin.
I could no sooner dissect my country
from my pupils, than disconnect the veins
that run through my heart.

This love is expensive.
Still I ask from others
what I can barely afford to give myself:
Touch me gently with voice and eyes
and hands that long to learn me.
Tell me that if I become more than who I am now,
your love will grow to match.

MY DARKNESS SHINES

by Jerrell Davis

My locs hang low and long
as my skin glows Black and strong

while I march thru crowds
of "well-intentioned" (yet, unWoke) White folk

who don't see their silence as violence
[ringing so loud]
they can't hear Truth in the quiet—

This steady diet of lies
sees my Light lost like dilated eyes:
amidst the dim of mind
My Darkness Shines!

FOLKS OF GREAT FORTUNE

By Lavon Ford

For me this life is not a game, it can be dangerous, it can be special, and it can be
absolutely wonderful; but it is a collision course controlled it seems by the

evil powers that be in total control, a token I think

to want to destroy people like me, my family, and society as a whole.

I really wonder how that could be.

History has taught me I am the realest man because anytime the strong in time prey
on the weak it's a disgraceful thing

no matter how much mistakes I do make trying to impress upon you my fate of
goodwill

you isn't no better than me as a bigger shyster.

I can't be getting angry at common folk who continue to tell me I owe you.

What is it! I reiterate I owe you what because

no one thing I does can make you feel better; except for in my death

I won't be around no more to make you remember,

what you were made to forget. Now it's time to break

the bottles open and celebrate being misunderstood folks

Because it feels good to say hooray, we've already won the battle.

I am indeed a folk of great fortune because I can turn

the source of weakness around and make

this disadvantage my strength over and over because I am stronger.

I don't want to resort to senseless violence ever,

if I don't have to; I just waste my energy trying to

prove what already many men and woman of my generation

like already tried to ask for freedom both tragedy and turmoil.

Yet one thing that I do know those hear me. Sure it appear so,
but you are not really in control as so you hoped all along.

Ask yourself or another person in you group if your folks
were originally so in control today, then why are them folks
spending billions of dollars trying to do away with a race folks
who just keep getting born again and again since the beginning of the
source.

So...

Today I stick with promoting unity now a day
because drama is too much to a burden to bear.
And money is definitely not worth dying to obtain,
burning bridges, or betraying friends, associates and family.
Before when there was more than enough
wealth in the economy, yet these folks in reality
whom have advance on the backs of wealth in the world do not want to
share all that glory, but none of us own it
that is why from the cradle to the grave we all go,
and diamond necklaces can poison a weak soul
then people started to throw each
other under the bus, arguing, backbiting,
and fighting with each other over absolutely nothing worth fighting for.

I wonder if now that these hard times as real
as they think that they are going to get
because even now we can see examine
what the source of bigots can bring to the table

absolutely nothing but harm, pity, and shame

My question is do to all the greed and false hope,

witchcraft being distributed down the pipeline of broken promises ever get old.

I think about how can I help those folks,

who get offered a little something like hope,

and they can use a little bit more relief in their lives threshold.

Though and though by granted the free gift of both hope and compassion this can give them the right approach

to strive not to be so petty or bitter.

So them and me, you can start to appreciate

the unseen lord's glory, as the greatest gifts to reward

they come for free things like hugs, smiles, friends, kisses, family,

sleeping, love, laughter, good memories.

Please keep each other in mind as we join this struggle

to endure and survive the greatest evil times of our lives

just like our associates can do.

To give a little more to someone else

whose lives in need is so special, that it helped, boosted us up

though times of both tragedy and turmoil as a grateful people.

As well as assisted developing a cool code of virtues.

For ethnics, religion, or race form showing a real love for humanity and people of all colors;

so I wrote this for whomever reads this shall see,

that you can truly believe and become some folks of great fortune.

The Narrow Path

by Gabriella Duncan

As I walked the winding path,
My breath was shallow
And anger was at times
My only friend ...

As I walked the narrow path
I felt alone and tired
I felt misunderstood ...

As I walked the narrow path
I craved deliverance from
Myself destruction ...

As I walked the narrow path
Dreams evaded my eyes
And anger created emptiness

Then
I saw you there
Right beside me
And realized

The path had always been
Wide enough for two
And I had never been alone

As I walked the narrow path.

Pondering Sky

by Matt Aspin

The sky
Don't look like it should

At night the light blocks out the scenes of the fight
Between the dark and light
The wrong and the right
Steals away the wonder and the might

Replaced with safe and secure
Hypnotized sparkling nothing allure of the quick and easy obscure.

So empty
Void of the pure

We need a new goal
The soul

A wonder serene
A new scene with questions that mean
We can still wonder at the sky with a few more secrets to share
Unaware with no care of the here and the there
And the why and the where
And the why out there
And the why do we care?

To wonder
To dare
To question unknown

The point of it all

Still not clear

Back to ponder

All night at the sky with just enough light to wonder

And dream

And to write

AQUATIC SPIRITS

By Minnie A. Collins

Across streams, inlets, lakes and rivers,

Dancing, leaping against the tidal upstream

Navigating the signs, currents, and ways of knowing,

Mapping and threading ancestral stories, unheard, unnoticed or ignored, of
lives captured in red, blue, green, gold and onyx gem stones

Now white washed, beached, sun bleached, adrift, aground

Soon smashed and graded by fields of asphalt spit

Aquatic Spirits jostle currents of ebb and flow seeking balance

While like a Janus spirit delve into the future and the past

Pondering DOT zones, housing codes, taxes, and waste water

Aquatic Spirits crack, quake, quaver ,amid squalls yet never quit

Restrain us if you think you can; Our spirits run with subterranean tides
on deeper fathoms.

COUNT ALL

by Gui Jean-Paul Chevalier

All here,
Without-beside locked walls,
Within, at barricade heart,
All absent matter.

A flash out of sight will stand on blocks of rusty time
Multitude risen, like the burns of scraped collective
Behave not to stand but watch,
Exist not to guard the evidence of counted year.
To justify memory,
We won't attend stagnant presence: All here, in with, to build

TUMOR

By Leija Farr

His country is a toiletry
Where people wipe dirty fingers
It is an oil stain on the map
In constant comparison to unwashed forks

His country wants badly to be cleaned
It strips itself nude at the bathtub
Wants to soak in soap suds and Epsom salt

It knows war by bloody hand prints
From Pollution
Crippled by pipe exhaust and tobacco

What will kill you faster?
The cancer of the throat or the cancer of hate?
A tumor modeled by a barrel, in your throat.

Unsanitary
It has been in the mouths of many others
Crust with vomit and wet prayer
The sidewalks drown in bowel movements

A country nicknamed toiletry
Nicknamed baby wipe
Where no one begins clean

OPPOSITES ATTRACT

By Lee Baldinger

Men are hard, women are soft

And that's not just in bed

Without women

Men become cold, brittle, cruel

Start lookin' for another guy to duel

Hard needs soft

And soft don't mean weak

In this dictionary

It's just another word for unique

Roles can be reversed

But not our nature

Yin and yang

Tears and toys

Flowers and monster trucks

What's going on?

There's fifteen per cent more blood flow in a woman's brain

Women's brains have more gray matter

Where information processing is done

The male brain is white matter dominant

Meaning more physical action

The male brain possesses fewer neural pathways

To and from the brain's emotion centers

In one year, a woman can give birth once

In one year, a man can produce enough sperm

To impregnate every single woman on earth

If we gave this science lesson as a test

Everyone would fail it

Even if it were an open book test

Everyone would fail it

Because men and women have different answers

Yin and yang

Tears and toys

Flowers and monster trucks

Is it any wonder the divorce rate is through the roof?

That in most relationships, someone becomes aloof?

But if we see each other as who we actually are

Maybe our behavior won't seem so bizarre

And we can hit a higher percentage of our shots

Cause we ought to be together

We've got to be together

Hard needs soft

And soft don't mean weak

In this dictionary

It's just another word for unique

Romeo and Julia

By Jerrell Davis

Stuck in a moment
Whose recognition causes it to slip away
Stuck in the ecstasy
of you next to me , inspecting every inch that you're lettin me,
Definitely setting us up for the agony.

A love that burns like April 20,
Fire burning, leaving our emotions bare—
I stare into your eyes,
I can't see myself and I wonder whether that's good or bad
But through it all you've been right there.

We grow
because of an image
Illustrating our respective blueprints of the future
Into a war that neither of us want to but must fight in.

We create a reality unfamiliar to each other
An emotional caste system that does nothing beyond breaking hearts-

Causing inevitable reform
when our hope underwhelms us,

See, someone's gotta lose
The question remains,
does fate choose?

LANGUAGE OF LOVE

By Marcus Harrison Green

There are days so unbelievably perfect that if life just relented a little in hoarding them there would never exist a reason to do drugs. From sunrise to the yellow orb's setting, what usually exist as fantasy or chemically enhanced delusion is somehow suffused into your life. For one day all your desires are accommodated. Your heart brims. Your belly burst. And laughter is played on a loop. Those days are ones you wish you could bottle portions of to spray as needed when the fetid aroma from the vast majority of 24 hour increments we experience surfaces to life.

Those days are ones that are so damn good that they start to stir panic. You gradually begin to realize that someone must have fallen comatose on the job and it can only be a matter of time before the world inevitably repairs whatever glitch that unwittingly released utopia from its cell.

The last day I had like that was the last day I saw you. You reminded the world — at least mine — that it was still engaged to reality and had to end its brief affair with the fantastical. I cut a productive work day short to greet you on a beachfront pew, with a view so divine of the Pacific it gave whoever sat there the impression it was their private lagoon. Nothing could have been more… perfect. But all it took was four fatal words — "We need to talk…" — for the Earth to screech to a halt so abrupt that half its population should still be stranded on Saturn's rings.

I should have known. To be so idiotic as to not see it coming. I immediately picked up your usage of a language I had long ago vowed to never speak again. Finding myself now forced with its fluency, I braced that organ in my chest that looks like an upside down pear for impact and said, "Okay" as if clueless about the volley coming next.

You went through a maze of words in order to finally find one, "friends," and championed it as if pawning off a consolation prize as first place. The language labored to come back to me and I remembered this term meant: "I can give you everything you never asked for and nothing that you want."

My intended reply was to tell you that I desired to be the first person you called on the shittiest of shitty days, and the sanctuary you ran to to from the swirling chaos that is most often referred to as life. I wanted to be, "your best ever" and give you the best ever, in sickness, in health, and all the other shit they said when I should have been paying more attention during the slices of those events I labeled as an affront to freedom and vowed to never participate in myself. Now the role you wanted me to play I seemed miscast for, but you thought I'd be perfect as my own jailer, in confinement to a boundary that would poise little danger to your muddled emotions. Something got lost in the translation of my protest and it came out: "Sure, I'd like that."

You aggravated my struggles with the jargon that much more when you said: "Are you okay?" which I recalled from my past dealings with the vernacular as a tricky phrase. Though stated as a question, it actually functioned as a statement that not loosely implied, "I need you to be okay with this."

While I wanted to shout so loudly that it shattered the sky: "No! How the fuck could I be! You painted a portrait of us that I can't unsee — with splashes of a nervous proposal, broad strokes of a wedding, and the contours of a child whose mother's name serves as her middle. What seemed real was revealed as forgery.

And so I uttered a response that had just as much to do with pride as linguistic mastery when I told you, "Of course I am."

You exhaled a heavy sigh — newly exonerated from a crime you were guilty of — and your demeanor immediately shifted to someone running late for a rendezvous with the rest of her life.

But just then words infected my head that were sure to lend me the tools to call you a coward for your unwillingness to take a risks on us, all while demanding I do the impossible — to stop in mid-soar after you propelled me and somehow not plummet. If I somehow emerged intact from my crash, you then asked me not to follow you even though you intended to leave bread crumbs behind. Somehow all those words were distilled down into just three whose misinterpretation proved impossible — and that only one other had ever heard me speak.

You paused and made sure to avoid my eyes in reaction to the obvious. The words I never said to anyone, you simply said were, "sweet." Your unfamiliarity with the language was evident. There could be no other reason other than sadism that you would have spewed one of its most malicious phrases, when "I engaged in lurid, prolonged sexual congress with your best friend, father, and optometrist within minutes of each other and then participated in a mass orgy with every single one of your co-workers and their extended circle that included canines, felines, wildebeest and their amphibian counterparts all in the same night!" would have been much more eloquent.

"Sweet" diminished all it took over half a lifetime to tell you into a 3rd grader with a cuddly crush on his teacher, whose homemade, back packed baked sugar cookie is received with a cheap smile and a quick dispatch to the trash can.

And for all that I ended my longstanding truce with something I prayed to never battle again. All this because you seemed to be the answer to "Why try again?"

That was what I was left with when all words had abandoned me except, "See you around," which is a version of goodbye that comes gift wrapped in a pretty package to dull the disappointment of what it encases.

I waited for a moment to try and let your presence evaporate, as alone as lonely allows. Some other fool had officially been shuttled off to the world I inhabited in previous months, that magical planet where you are teased with euphoria before being banished back to the same cold rock everyone else resides. Eyes that once sparkled at your sight now drowned in an ocean more abyssal than the one that never did belong to us. I said aloud, "I won't miss her … I never loved her," but of course that too came out all wrong.

The Last Breaths of the Day

by Matt Aspin

I just experienced the earth's last breath of the day

White noise, leaves rustling, endless, monotonous hypnotic

Then slower, and slower, and then, subtly and suddenly, silence

Overwhelming, deafening, still... silence

Less than a minute, then another breath

Rustling, deep, full, then receding, and then again, silence

In and out

The last breaths of her day

Did you miss it?

Slow down to her pace

All is done

All is in balance

Tomorrow is another day

The Cracked Window

By Georgia S. McDade

The cracked window for good things black is closing.
The young American-African president born in the USA
    opened the window wider than ever before.
But the opening is still a mere crack.
The young president could not, did not
    open the window wide; he did the best he could: he
    increased the size of the crack.
His and the hard work of many others cracked this window
    but only for a short time.
Eight years cannot possibly repair, rectify the centuries of lost,
    stolen history, rectify the murderous behavior.
Almost any attempt to do good was met with powerful opposition
    as the rich got richer and the poor got poorer.
Many tried and still try their best to close and keep the window
    closed.
The window closes—the size of the crack decreases—in less
    than a year unless we work extremely hard to keep it
    open.
Through this cracked window came light that afforded many
    a sight they had never before seen.
Their exposure to black life was real and broad.
No longer did they see only the millionaire stars,
    "personalities," and athletes, that infinitesimal group
    many—from the man on the street to Supreme Court
    justices—choose to use as proof affirmative action is no
    longer necessary.

For the first time, many saw the conflict between the masses,
      the everyday people and police, could understand the
      negative attitudes of so many blacks, browns all over
      the land.
Fearing for their lives, police officers mowed down citizens
      as young as twelve and as old as ninety-three, the innocent and the ill.
Rarely was one bullet adequate to stop a black person,
      always guilty 'til proven innocent.
Rarely was a policeman indicted; forget the word
      "convicted" though occasionally the aggrieved collected
      taxpayer money.
For the first time, others saw what many blacks had seen
      for centuries.
For the first time a record of the number of citizens killed
      by police is being kept though all police are not always
      using the same standard.
A centuries'-old cry should be resurrected: No taxation
      without representation.
"Occupy" became the call word.
No New Jim Crow became a mantra.
Black Lives Matter, no too or also necessary.
Demonstrate constantly that this is the case.
Many of every color profess and protest constantly.

So show whatever needs to be shown through the window
      these last few months.

Get more poems, novels, and plays in any form you choose.

Get more slave narratives published and filmed, more

Butlers, 42s, Fruitvales, and Comptons.

Get more songs, paintings, music, and dance.

Get more Coateses and Pittses, more Herberts in print.

Get more news stories of the horrors, inconsistences, unfairness.

Get more voters registered, of course!

But get more registered voters to vote!

Get more winning, honest, responsible candidates.

Speak truth; speak truth in your way.

Give details.

Know that Joy DeGruy named "the problem" Post-Traumatic-

Slave Syndrome in 2005, when the crack was much smaller.

Know that blacks are not the only ones afflicted with the

dis-ease.

This dis-ease eats all of us, some at a much faster, more ravishing

pace than others.

Know that enclosing persons—yes, persons, human beings—

in cages rather than houses, good jails rather than good

schools makes folks act less than human and not

the God-created beings they are.

Remember: only the size of the crack is a bit larger.

We can do our best to keep the crack open by learning

from the exposure.

Or we can suffer more negative consequences of the crack's
   narrowing, if not disappearing.

We need that light.

We—all of us—can do the uncomfortable and the inconvenient, everything
   to put out the fires engendered by this closing of the crack; we can
   make the crack sufficiently wider soon.

OR WE CAN HAVE OUR HANDS FILLED WITH
   BATTLING THE FIRE NEXT TIME.

The Less You Talk

By Luke Roehl

The less you talk
the more you hear,
mind is focused,
heart is clear.
Words are few
and strong when said,
connected from the heart
the hands
the head.
We're taught to ought
that Loud is life,
while Quiet goes about working
and spreading
light.

RAINER BEACH

By Larry Crist

It's a neighborhoody kind of place,
folksy with little trace of that same decay
we left in the north end part of town.
There's noodles and Pho and King Donuts
alongside teriyaki as well as all the usual
standard eating choices, a library
and mortuary and Safeway behind
the corner veterinarian sporting separate
entrances for dog or cat. Where no one
race dominates: brown, black,
Asian, Mexican, African, Euro descendants,
Baptists, Moslems, infidels like me
who wander these lightly littered streets
in relative harmony

Lots of sirens, an occasional gun-shot,
car alarms and yappy dogs, muscle-cars
with jacked-up chassis, shrill engines,
thin tires, bright colors, shiny chrome.
They roam up and down our road, as
I gaze out the window down our street
past tree-sized cactus to the water
and Rainier Beach High, home of the Vikings

As a descendant Viking i'm eager to attend
one of these games. I'd check if there were Vikings
in the bleachers, or on the field, raiding from the
water — The water, blue today like the sky, our
neighborhood crows i toss 'em scraps
onto the next roof over, and watch as they
join the greater rush hour collective, south
toward Renton, where Hendrix still lives
down from Bruce Lee's, north of here

Here — where I am happy to be, Rainier
Beach, in such live and rarified company

TRUCE FOR A WARZONE

By Kayla Blau

When her body became a warzone,

I sat wobbly-kneed in Dr. Smith's sterilized walls, pretending to color.

He had all types of schemes and weapons and missiles to launch

inside my mother's body.

To fight the bad guys.

This is how we conceptualized it together;

Me, all stringy hair and loose teeth,

Her, fuzzy scalp and aching bones

I like to think this juvenile explanation helped her too.

That the wartorn cells and casualties of chemo

Came to mean more than just survival.

She fought the urge to become a prisoner inside her own body,

This will kill the rapidly dividing poisonous cells, but may kill some
   healthy ones too

inside her own mind,

You have six to nine months to live (have I taken this pill yet today?)

inside her own home,

Mommy doesn't want to be sick anymore, sweetheart

When the time came, my mother flew no white flag.

She offered no truce, showed not an ounce of defeat.

Two years past the doctor's expiration date,

she left with grace.

I refuse to accept that she "lost her battle."

She simply won unconventionally.

She was taken after summer's storm

Pulled, the blues of her eyes

She, her — it's foreign to refer to mother

so informally now,

like

present

tense

Questions to the waves of her grave like

"When did you know love?"

"The blue dress or the black one?"

"What'd you think of the war — all of them?

Did you march in Vietnam protests or roll your eyes?"

When did your bitten tongue turn light gold?

Instead,

I recall the way in which she folded towels,

crease out in the closet,

so we could grab one readily, she explained,

for an impromptu trip to the lake or

whoosh

how she splayed warm sheets over my giggling limbs,

freshly cleansed, still warm,

Like I thought her cheek would be

As I kissed her tomb

Goodbye

The atypical cells divided & attacked

No amount of pink ribbons

Or celebrity endorsements

Can call truce for that

Hours in white-walled holding cells,

holding our breath,

holding hands,

holding it together,

not even fooling ourselves

Cancer became a swear word

Whispered between relatives like the plague

Shushed into silence like it would stop spreading that way

It spread anyway.

Submission, remission, readmission

When hospital beds become familiar

Scans, biopsies, blood tests

When the nurse sneaks you extra pudding

"for being so patient"

When your blood's blood is victim and all you can be is

Patient.

Not Far From Lake Tahoe—
& then, in Many Parts of South Seattle

By Jeanne Morel

Clowns wear masks seemingly in high spirits. — *Zhang Shuguang*

the ski hill licks the dribs of birds

where do you come from—I come from the sky

Gnostics pass songs on lodgepole

pines

sap the sap runs dry

the sky reaches to California

tram mart

white folks search

Reddit for authentic ethnic rest /aurants

slurp ramen and ginger

mules amid the cranes that rise excavated lots and blocks birds of the apoca/

lypse

or / not

— alternate days coo over the enjera —

proposed land use a 6-story structure with 44 residential units above retail

surface parking for 4 vehicles

existing structure to be

demolished

post offices down out & disappearing no possibility of return /

/ elsewhere

Va a Llover (it Will Rain)

By ReLL Be Free

When chickens come to roost, you expect it.

When the lies become your truth, that's a death wish-

Not jus for you

but even me too

Because you'll only have destruction on your checklist.

Check it—

A lot people keepin heaters in their cellars

Anybody can contribute to the weather

Cuz whenever people pull it

and the street is raining bullets

For protection need more than an umbrella, fareal

The steel kills like pullin jobs out the steel mills

If you ain't invest, tough one (Teflon), you will feel

Precipitation, complacent with devastation

Like Flint Michigan

How the water works is a real deal

Break—

I got a sixth sense about this shit, cuz I seent it before

I've flipped thru pages and pages of complacent phases of history that
stuck together thru centuries and ages

The foolish consider the '60s the pinnacle of race relations

Den of thieves,

Land of Thebes,

They blame our sins then trained our sons into the saddest of gladiators

Pitting brothers against each other for their entertainment in this
generation's Coliseum

Call it the news, or the NBA, or the NFL

Or the prisons,

cuz jus like justice for us there's no buy jus cell (sell)

In Guatemala they taught me "va a llover"

When you watch the sky rise you can predict the fall

While the empire stands tall like the Taj Mahal or cathedral halls

The evil calls from the leaders stall and stifle all progress toward equity
out of antiquity

Cuz the real savages are the ones stuck in the past

Holding onto the grasp of their forefathers who steal, kill and destroy

No wonder they're raising hell, jus like their parents raised them to be

I knew these truths to be self evident and the lessons never fading from me

If the feds ever waiting (weighting) for me it's gon be a heavy cost

I know my environment, inspired by the spirit

I believe I got the leaves of the trees on my side

I got the seeds of belief in my eyes pushing and looking thru debacles
forward to the destination, the Freedom colored finish line

They recruit new cops (modern day slave catchers) to cater their twisted fear,

Using German Shepherds and water hoses in collaboration with their hate in
attempt to turn our Blackness blank

But they made a mistake to take our blindness for weakness

We walk in the steps of Douglass, once we learn that poverty is the opposite
of Justice

We gon pursue it with all hustle and muscle

Expecting a struggle but we been fighting for ever

So when that Black Fist go up, and that white house come down

And the victory drum sounds

That's the Living Water cycle:

What goes around comes around

OUR MOTHER

By Minnie A Collins

She cries, weeps, cannot be consoled
Her artery is pierced; heart is pleading
Asking us to honor her, respect her, love her…

She grimaces yet tries to smile between pulses and gushes of energy
Her heart soon flat lines
As we core into her depths, weaken the sub stratasphere, gouge out her body
She asks, "How much longer must I suffer and be pain?"

Who is to blame?
Who wrote the policies? Who are the developers?
Who dug too deeply?
Disclaimers, ignored, forgotten, soon useless, swirl

We have invaded our Mother's heart, foreclosed on our earth homes
No bank can buy us out, board us up, or tempt new buyers at one percent

Will our Mother relent, forgive us for our war on Her?

A war on our Mother is unpredictable. She may allow us to win a skirmish
But not before unleashing Her Supreme forces: drought, tornadoes,
    hurricanes, 40 days and nights of rain, eruptions, tidal waves and fear.

Will She relent and forgive?

RECESSITATE

By Tymon Haskins

I lay there

I look at the world and media

my body is portrayed lifeless as less life that lessens the life that was given
value before time

Recessitate me

Institutional racism, unfunded schools, deprived families

Shade my eyes and flood my heart with pain that cover the hope. Like dark
cloud cover the sky the systemic issues cover

Recessitate this body breathe

My heart is broken

Like Glass in many pieces

Shattered from the racism

Recessitate, breath, breath

Struck by the images of Medgar Evers

Shattered by the tyranny that demanded an Underground Railroad

Unmendable

Gasping from the pain of a mist old history

Recessitate, breath, breath,

My body covered by the dark blankets of segregation, covering the pain,
   covering the scars, and smothering the expectations

Recessitate, breathing, breathing

Dreams awakened by the light of freedom
Dreams breathing life through veins of the African heritage that was taken away

Recessitate eyes opened to my true heritage
Eyes open to who I am
Eyes who opened to to the one who loved me first

Breathing gasping
Hope infused in this brown to strengthening those who are broken, Arnold,
   terminating the injustices
Speaking to the hearts about love

Recessitate, living, my eyes open

My breath is life through my viens but life too many
I can see

I am breathing
Living
Breathing

TRIMMING ROSES FOR A VASE,
I SCISSOR THROUGH MY FINGER

By T. Clear

Stolen from a shrub
crowding the sidewalk
on Dawson Street,
it's no surprise
that I pay in blood,
the tidy skin-slit
dripping corpuscles.
How could I expect
to slip them secretly
from a stranger's garden
without a price,
the sprig tucked smugly
into my sack?

Atonement is measured
                in layers of gauze
            and a finger looped in tape.

FROM THE UTILITY MUFFIN RESEARCH KITCHEN
(FOR FZ)

By Paul Nelson

From the Utility Muffin Research Kitchen
we bring you *Watermelon in Easter Hay.*
We bring you Hey nana Hey nana Hey nana Hey,
   Hoy! Hoy! Hoy!

We bring you the latent clay brain
droppings of Bruce Bickford. Bring you
            Black Napkins. Bring you Vinnie Colaiuta
            kinda young kinda wow!

            From the Utility Muffin Research Kitchen
      we bring you *Sofa No. 1,* bring you *Sheik
Yerbouti,* bring you *Ship Arriving Too Late
      to Save a Drowning Witch.*

            We bring you Jean-Luc Ponty and *Inca Roads,*
      George Duke and *the slime oozing out of your
      TV set.* Bring you Ruth Underwood, no commercial potential
& Jimmy Carl Black, the *Indian of the group.*

            From *Shut Up and Play Your Guitar* we bring you
      Trouble Every Day, bring you *Lumpy Gravy* bring
      you *hair growing out every ho-le in me. Hey nana
      Hey nana Hey nana Hey, Hoy! Hoy! Hoy!*

From Live at the Roxy And Elsewhere we bring you
            Montana, bring you *Camarillo Brillo where he was
                  breeding a dwarf but he wasn't done yet,* bring you *a
      fuming incense stencher by where she hung her castanets.*

We bring you groupies and prostate cancer and *Hey,*
I'll buy you a pizza, bring you *a stratocaster with a*
whammy bar and the most wicked guitar this side
of Jimi. Bring you *acerbic, uncompromising, clinical*

bring you *theatrical, brash* and *wry,* bring you *lusty, energetic,*
sardonic and *provocative.* Bring you giraffes ejaculating whipped
cream, Marines in unintentional anti-war performance
at the Garrick Theater & *the toads of the short forest.*

From *Jazz From Hell* bring you *Moon Unit,* Dweezil,
Ahmet and Diva and Italian, French, Sicilian, Greek, Arab
blues guitar filtered through Edgard Varèse, Igor Stravinsky, and
Anton Webern, w/ a dash of Johnny Guitar Watson.

Bring you this to poke-you-&-stroke-you-til-his-wrist-gets-numb,
til you're home on the sofa lodged on the way to Mars in some
unnamed constellation. Bring you music as religion and one who'd
predicted the U.S. fascist theocracy til December 4, '93,

for one final tour, on a cloud of cigarette smoke, as an   extinct   mollusk,
        jellyfish, a genus of gobiid fishes, a metazoan fossil and an asteroid,
as a gene in the bacterium that causes urinary tract infections because that's
why it hurts when you pee, waiting for one more VD shot on Sofa No. 3.

II.

Art

"Dasha D" Victor Straube

"Letter" Victor Straube

"Blossoms" Victor Straube

"Dance With Me" Victor Straube

III.

PROSE

Georgia Stewart McDade:
A Life Mightier Than Obstacles

by Sharon H. Chang

Georgia Stewart McDade has a mind bigger than the world and yet she is so easy to be around. Warm, friendly, full of smiles and stories, she's irresistibly energetic and far younger than her years. Don't be fooled though—cause she's fierce as anything too. She is a Black woman who grew up in the segregated south, trail-blazed her entire life and doesn't plan on slowing down any time soon. Georgia is the first African American woman to earn a Ph. D. in English from the University of Washington. In addition to being a college educator for three decades she is a prolific poet and writer, has published three books, once traveled the world in six months, and is headed to Malawi for the first time where she will lecture at two universities. Oh. And she just turned 70.

Georgia was born in 1945 in Louisiana, the middle of eight children. Not the oldest, not the youngest, she laughingly says she started writing because nobody would listen. "You know I'd write when I got upset or I couldn't get to my mom cause somebody else was there," she recalled. "I'd just go in a room or under a tree and just write ... I just loved telling stories." She grew up in a shotgun house in Monroe during Jim Crow. "Of course it was segregated," she said. "We were poor. My mom used to cook three slices of bacon for five children. I didn't have a whole slice of bacon until I went to college." Georgia's mother was a maid who earned $3.50 a day. Georgia's father was a laborer who couldn't always find work. But Georgia won't spend too much time on any of this because, she explains, being poor did not define her.

"I don't remember thinking 'Oh I'm poor' you know?" she elaborates. "And luckily I was in a situation where my theory was that it wouldn't always be that way." Instead she reminisces tenderly about walking with her mother to church, her father driving her to school every day, her oldest brother being the only person who could trick her every April Fool's, and how everyone knew everyone else in Monroe. "Many of us were in the same school first through twelfth grade. Most of us grew up in the same house. We were there all of our lives. So we knew everybody in the neighborhood." She tells me to look up the poem "Nikki-Rosa" (1968) by Nikki Giovanni:

> ... they never understand
>
> Black love is Black wealth and they'll
>
> probably talk about my hard childhood
>
> and never understand that
>
> all the while I was quite happy.

Still the stark reality of living in a racist anti-Black society ever intruded. "I was eleven when I really learned about segregation," she says. The first day of seventh grade she proudly donned a green dress, boarded the bus, and plopped herself down in a front seat. An old Black woman in the back said, "Get up child you can't sit there." Georgia turned to her mother, "Why can't I sit up there Madea?" But her mother didn't answer. After getting off the bus Georgia asked again, "Madea, *why* couldn't I sit at the front?" Her mother still didn't answer. Georgia doesn't remember that school day but she recollects running straight to her mother after school insisting, "Madea, why couldn't I sit on that seat??" And finally her mother, face cloudy, answered, "Colored people can't sit in the front."

> *The world did not operate better because races*
> *were separate.*
> *But generations paid and pay horrendous prices*
> *because races were separate.*
>
> – George McDade, "The Nastiest Word"

With a determinedness that would become the theme of her life, young Georgia resolved firmly, "Well. I just won't ride the bus!" (she did not ride the bus again until college). She went on to excel in primary and then secondary school. As a high school freshman she was selected to take part in an honors program and colloquium every week. As a high school senior she was one of 42 students from nine states selected to participate in the first Black student National Science Foundation program at Grambling College. "They said we were high ability students," she recalls, "We took Biology, Chemistry, Physics and Math and [went] on field trips." Georgia graduated valedictorian of her class. She applied to eight colleges and universities and was accepted to all of them.

∽

Some of Georgia's high school teachers thought she might be successful as the first African American student to integrate Northeast Louisiana State University in Monroe (now University of Louisiana). Georgia set out to visit, "I was all excited." Her excitement was quickly squelched. Upon arriving she asked to see the dorms and a white woman working at the college coldly replied, "They told us we have to go to school with you. They never said we have to live with you." Georgia shakes her head with the memory. "We really thought that when the court said desegregate – you had to desegregate. Now we know better." But just like the determined little Black girl who had self-boycotted the bus at eleven years old, Georgia forged ahead again undaunted. "I thought, 'Well. I'm not going if I can't live on campus!'" she relays with a gleam in her eye. Instead Georgia studied English at Southern University in Baton Rouge, a historically Black university, where she had been offered a scholarship. After she earned her Bachelor of Arts in 1967 she went on to graduate school at Atlanta University—also a historically Black university—where again she was offered a scholarship. She earned her Master of Arts in 1971.

The first person to suggest she study English in college was appropriately a high school English teacher. But as a young student Georgia resisted. Certainly she had always loved reading and telling stories but to her, English was not literature. English meant diagramming sentences and parts of speech and she was convinced most people knew all the English they needed by the time they were in sixth grade. It wasn't until a world literature class her second year at Southern that a realization came to her. "I thought if *this* is English—I want in," Georgia beams. "I *loved* the university cause it had all of these courses."

～

Full of drive and ambition, Georgia was then accepted to the Ph.D. program at the University of Washington (UW). However unlike her experiences at Southern and Atlanta University which she mostly relays as positive, she has mixed feelings about her experience at UW which was predominantly white. She describes it as a "hard time". For instance, Georgia finished her coursework in reasonable time but tried to write her dissertation on Shakespeare for two years before someone finally thought to tell her she couldn't because too many scholars had already done so. Georgia headed to the offices of three different white English professors. "And all three of them said, 'Are you going to do [James] Baldwin or [Richard] Wright?' *All three*." Georgia remembered reflecting, "That's really odd. You would think they'd know more writers."

"You know you can stop," the English Department Chair advised her. "You don't have to go any further and you've still gone farther than anybody else has ever gone." But Georgia had never stopped nor did she intend to stop now. At last she sought out the only Black faculty she remembers in the English department, an African American woman, who told her to write on Jessie Fauset. "I never heard of Jessie Fauset,'" Georgia countered. The professor countered back, "*That's* why you do Jessie Fauset." Jessie Fauset was a Black woman author, editor, poet, educator and journalist who penned multiple poems, essays, four novels and was hired by W.E.B. Du Bois in 1919 to be the literary editor of his magazine *The*

Crisis. Georgia wrote a 260-page dissertation entitled, "From Hopeful to Hopeless: Three Novels of Jessie Fauset."

She earned her Ph. D. in 1987.

Mid-dissertation Georgia had heard that Tacoma Community College (TCC) was looking for an English teacher. "I never thought of myself as a writer, I just wrote," she says, "But I always wanted to teach." In fact it was way back in Monroe as a resolute little girl that Georgia set that definitive goal and (in typical Georgia style) never once changed her mind. "I must've been about five or six [years old] when I decided I wanted to teach," she smiles. "Every year I wanted to teach the grade I was in." Finally she decided she wanted to teach college. A high school counselor objected, "There's no college where you can teach!" But, Georgia says, "I knew enough ... and just sort of ignored him." That gleam has crept back into her eyes.

> *I don't tackle all obstacles.*
> *I do not believe in wasting energy.*
> *Some obstacles I leave alone.*
> *Other obstacles I go around.*
> *Some obstacles I stare down.*
>
> *– Georgia McDade, "Obstacles"*

She applied for the position and got the job. Though, of course, racism kept encroaching. "There were people at TCC who wouldn't take my class because I'm Black," she said. Clearly higher education and Seattle were no more immune to anti-Blackness than her native Deep South. When she first came to Seattle, Georgia says, she rode the bus downtown, saw Black men with white women. "I *never* saw that in Monroe and I just wanted to bring everybody from Monroe, Louisiana, to Seattle." But after she had been out here about a month, Georgia laughs, she wanted to take everyone from Seattle back to Monroe. "People here [in the Northwest] will tell you in a minute that there's no racism; there's no prejudice," she remarks, but that perception is dangerously false.

But plainly racism was nothing new and had been a constant through the prose of her life. Despite the discrimination Georgia loved her teaching position and stayed committed at Tacoma Community College for three decades while continuing to live in Seattle. "I had students who said I shouldn't be teaching in Seattle. I should go back and help people in the south," Georgia notes. "I always said there are a lot of people in the south who can help people in the south. It's the people out here [who need help]." And true to her word (aside from the time she traveled thirty-two countries in six months) she's been here ever since.

Today Georgia still lives in her South Seattle home with her brother and sister. A co-founder and charter member of the African American Writers' Alliance (AAWA), Georgia began reading her writings in public in 1991. Her works include *Travel Tips for Dream Trips*, questions and answers about her six-month, solo trip around the world; *Outside the Cave* and *Outside the Cave II*, collections of poetry; and numerous essays, stories, and other poems. She just held a huge 70th birthday party in which she divided her life into acts. The first act was Monroe where she was born. The second act was Southern University in Baton Rouge 189 miles away where she went to college. The third act was Seattle, Tacoma. "The fourth act," she clasps her hands, "was the world where I put all of my travels. And the fifth act? Is now ..."

> *I am the narrator*
>
> *I write.*
>
> *I rule.*

> *– Georgia McDade, "My Poems"*

Sharon H Chang has worked with young children and families for over a decade as a teacher, administrator, advocate and parent educator. She is currently a writer, scholar and activist who focuses on racism, social justice and the Asian American diaspora with a feminist lens. Her pieces have appeared in BuzzFeed, ThinkProgress, Hyphen Magazine ParentMap Magazine, The Seattle Globalist, AAPI Voices and International Examiner. She also serves as a consultant for Families of Color Seattle and is on the planning committee for the Critical Mixed Race Studies Conference.

INESCAPABLE WHITENESS

By Marilee Jolin

I never really wanted to be White. Until I was 10 I didn't even realize that's what I was. When people talked about race I assumed they meant ethnic heritage which seemed like a separate issue from the color of one's skin. I understood myself to be Italian and Swedish—¼ of each. I'd proudly claim those two identities and feel pity for my friends who were only and 1/8 or 1/16 of something or—worst of all—didn't claim anything at all.

This all came to mind when I attended the European Dissent Community Meeting last Saturday. The meeting was an opportunity for White people interested in anti-racism work to come together. I was pleasantly surprised to learn that, rather than rallying us for immediate action or flaunting their activist successes, this meeting was focused on building relationships and fostering the inner work necessary for White people seeking racial justice.

The leaders spoke of "internalized racial superiority" and encouraged us to reflect on our lives through the lens of race. We were split into groups and offered three questions to ponder and then discuss: 1) When did you first become aware of racism and want to do something about it? 2) How have you worked with other white people? And 3) When did you become white?

That last question really stuck in my mind. As I mapped out my "race history" in response to these questions I was reminded of how strongly I identified as Italian and Swedish as a child and with what embarrassment—shame, even—I realized that these European roots did not count as my race.

It was around 3rd grade that I learned the more important labels people around me used: Mexican; Native; and of course, Black. I specifically remember Joshtone: the one Black kid in our whole school, from the one Black family in our tiny Eastern Washington town. It quickly became clear to me that Joshtone's race was significant in a way mine was not. Joshtone and the Mexican kids and especially the Native kids had an interesting and somewhat dangerous claim to race that I did not even though my Noni cooked polenta and commanded us to "Manja! Manja!" at dinner.

I remember filling in the circle next to "White (non-Hispanic)" on my first standardized test in 4th grade. I scratched that #2 pencil begrudgingly, dark graphite smudges transferring to the back of my hand, frustrated at claiming White as my identity. Even in 4th grade I had some sense of the terrible legacy of being White. Even then, I longed to distance myself from the color of slavery and small-pox blankets and segregation. I preferred manicotti and lutefisk, for sure.

On our way to the meeting last Saturday, my father-in-law asked me for more information on European Dissent so I read the mission statement to him as we drove. One sentence stood out powerfully to me: "We are persons of European descent who recognize that our varying ethnic histories have been *forged into a common White identity in order to nurture and sustain racism* (emphasis mine).

In reading this, something clicked for me. Whiteness, they were saying, is not a race into which I was born, but an identity created by a racist system into which I've been co-opted. I'm only White because at some point it was advantageous to include the Italians (who had previously been discriminated against and relegated to less-desirable real estate) in order to continue powerfully excluding the real danger—Blacks.

The next book on my reading list is "The History of White People" by Nell Irvin Painter. A Salon interview of the author captured my attention and returned these fascinating tidbits:

- The term "Caucasian" originated in 1795; created by a scientist seeking to find the "most beautiful race" of people

- There have been 3 major "expansions" of Whiteness in the United States, the first shifting suffrage from income to race (any "white" man could vote) the next two shifts incorporating immigrants (the Irish in the 19th century and the rest of the lighter skinned immigrants before WWII)

It kind of blew my mind to realize how much the "race" of White was created and sustained over the centuries. Thought up by a eugenicist, expanded to include "acceptable" immigrants, entirely to serve further racism and discrimination. Whiteness is, apparently, meaningless!

And yet, it's not. I cannot deny that being White in the United States has dramatically impacted my life. Whether I like it or not, whether it is accurate or not, my skin tone provides me with privileges, access and freedoms denied to others. My friends of color's lives have been dictated by the color of their skin as well. They have been pulled over disproportionately, suspended more, sentenced unequally, given fewer chances and had to jump higher hurdles. And that matters a great deal.

I can't get away from the racial construct in which my whiteness was born, however ill-fitting or historically inaccurate or maliciously created. I am a white person living in the United States and I must admit to how this has benefited me and protected me my whole life. I must also acknowledge how these benefits have shaped my internal framework for understanding myself and the world around me.

But I think I can also acknowledge that the imposition of whiteness has come from outside myself and does not fully describe me. In the same way that I can decry the evils of the Jim Crow system without denying the effects, I can also reject the racial binary imposed by those perpetuating racism while still taking to heart the ongoing harm both internal and external resulting from it.

I am learning to accept the reality of being white: how society has taught me whiteness is normal and everything else is an exotic or inferior minority; how I've been trained to notice skin color as the primary distinguisher between myself and others; how I still too often believe the solution to society's ills is for other people to become more like me. For all of this and so much more, I claim full complicity with my white identity. It is real. It has shaped me. I am now working hard to root out and exorcise these demons of racial superiority within me.

In this pursuit, I have many opportunities and excellent guides along this journey. I am excited to become more involved with the thoughtful, passionate, open-eyed and self-aware white folks I met at European Dissent. I am looking forward to the Dismantling Racism series coming up on June 11th. I am planning to attend the People's Institute Undoing Racism training on July 16-17. I have so much to learn, so much to un-learn and so much to do. And not a moment to lose.

White Allies, and Black Liberation

by Amir Islam

Ours is the story of two young men who grew up just miles apart similar in many ways, but with different paths. I have known Ben Haggerty *a.k.a.* Macklemore since our childhood days. We grew up together, and although not the best of friends we shared childhood memories, busted raps together, ran in some of the same circles, and later on in life we would keep up with each other, even crossing paths on our road to recovery from drug addiction.

We are both Seattle natives, both have a love for Hip-Hop, a love for art, and a love for the people. Macklemore went on to sell millions of records, and sell out arenas all around the world. While I ended up in and out of trouble, eventually finding my way out of prison, getting involved in black-led community organizing, and picking up arms to fight in the struggle for black liberation.

Recently Macklemore invited me to listen and critique his most controversial single yet, "White Privilege 2." We met up. We made small talk. He hit play. We listened ... Twice.

Almost immediately my trauma as a black man kicked in. Despite our similarities when I listened to the song, I felt our paths diverge. I felt conflicted knowing that despite his best intentions of dealing with his own privilege, and trying to be an ally, he would still come out as the victor of a war neither of us started, but that hasn't ended yet ... and our situation—myself, and other "descendants of slaves" would remain the same ... Even in their attempts at allyship the grandchildren of our oppressors continue to gain from our oppression. They will still make fortunes, and become icons off our dead bodies once again, while we continue to die every 48 hours at the hands of the fascist ass police.

While Black voices that have always mattered lament in the streets ...

"No justice, no peace ..."

As I listened to the song my mind was filled with the ways Macklemore and other white folks could actually do something about their privilege. Maybe he could buy a small piece of land in Africa & donate it to black folks call it 40 Acres and a mule land. I don't know call it freedom town. He could help use his resources to create space for black folks? He could donate to my freedom fund, and directly impact my life.

After all, wasn't I someone he could leverage the wealth inequality gap right back too? Black folks like me directly in his own backyard. Give us some resources so that we can catch up to him since my ancestors gave their lives unwillingly for his privilege.

I'm sure some of you are getting uncomfortable reading this. Whenever Black people talk about giving up some of that white privilege, that wealth, those resources that flow in such an abundance for white people and start talking about re-allocating it back to the people it was stolen from it get's kind of uncomfortable. It is hard for white people to give up their privilege. It's hard for anyone. Who wants to give up their power? And that's what privilege is. Power.

This is the lens of an everyday black man like me. This is the only lens I'm used to seeing things in.

"White Privilege 2" is a song that will engage people in lengthy debates about race, inequalities, and the white-supremacist-capitalist-patriarchy, but it's a conversation that is never ending. As I listened again I wondered if it would just be another song, maybe even a Grammy winner, or just another song that sparked yet another dead end conversation before business went on as usual.

The lyrics rang a truth that sounded so familiar "Go buy a big-ass lawn, go back to your big-ass house, get a big-ass fence, and keep people out." I found myself wondering if he would do exactly that. Macklemore could make off with this song, profit off our dead bodies, go back in that big ass house and we would still be dying in the streets while his privilege gets him yet another Grammy.

I questioned: "Will I be his partner in crime as he rides off in the sunset with more of our culture?"

The image kept replaying in my head of the lavish mansion fortress home of his, with him tip toeing like a burglar safely sliding back to his hide out with a big bag of appropriation. Him opening the door to a scene of white b-boys doing windmills, and air-flairs, and head spins all over his palace.

After all, he himself has proclaimed white folks appropriated our culture, marketed it, and capitalized off it so well. My mind thought "maybe he's the king of thieves, and this is his lair."

I told him all of this, and how I felt about the song and he thanked me, inviting me, and others to be a part of the community to hold him accountable, and to use this moment, and his platform as an organizing tool.

It's hard to trust the gratitude or the invitation. With good reason. Black folks are used to white America taking the very life from us, and capitalizing on our bodies, and appropriating our soul. Why should we be so trusting? Does the rape victim trust the rapist, no matter how friendly the face?

Black folks see that Japanese and Jewish people received reparations for crimes committed against them, and wonder why we have not been compensated as well. We are bewildered, and appalled that America has never corrected this grave injustice, and moral tragedy, and we will never feel at home here until it is corrected.

Have not our mothers given the very milk from their breast to nourish this nation literally giving it life while their own children have perished away? There is a difference between saying sorry and actually making an amends. Making an amends involves action. It means to do something right for the wrong you have committed against someone.

I'm thankful to have the opportunity to be included in this process, to be valued for my expertise around the subject matter. I'm grateful to be in this moment and help shape history, but my gratitude is tempered by my anger. Nothing changes the fact that so many countless black, and brown bodies have been oppressed, and killed. Their screams for freedom remain unanswered.

Will one, rich, powerful, famous white male voice still be centered and heard over the screams, and call to action liberation for the most marginalized and oppressed?

Ultimately this conversation on white privilege is necessary, but in order to move forward it must be accompanied by action. As Frederick Douglass once said: "Power concedes nothing without demand." It is time for our allied to join us in demanding that our nation/government provide reparations for slavery. We must find ways to directly compensate black people for our ancestor's contribution to the construction of this country and to balance huge wealth inequality directly made off the backs whites whipped it off.

Bernie Sanders just recently said no to reparations, yet "he marched with King." There can be no ally-ship without action.

I was a part of the Bernie Sanders interruption here in Seattle at Westlake, and hearing the hate that came out of the mouths of the "most progressive so called liberal white Americans" in 2016 makes me rejoice to the heavens that I played my part. I'm sure our ancestors are smiling down on us.

My real appeal is not to white America or the European. That is not my place. That is the work of my allies. My message is to all Africans throughout the diaspora. It is time for a "Black Magna Carta" it's time for liberation throughout the African diaspora. We know the white man will stay in a place of privilege for some time longer, but what are we going to do about it?

We must continue to divest, continue to resist, continue to interrupt, continue to change the narratives and push for our full freedom, and liberation. By any means necessary. We must continue the fight for black liberation.

BLACK DEATH

by Hodan Hassan

In the last couple of months, we've seen two black people murdered, both events recorded and widely distributed in traditional and social media. Alton Sterling was a black man living in Baton Rouge who was killed by the police on Tuesday July 5th. He was selling CD's outside of a store when the altercation happened, he was handcuffed and on the ground when he was murdered.

The police in Falcon Heights, MN killed Philando Castile on Wednesday, July 6th. He was pulled over by the police for an alleged traffic violation and disclosed he had weapon. He was reaching for his driver's license when the officer opened fire on him. His death was broadcast on Facebook Live™ by his girlfriend, who was a passenger in the car.

Just like many other black people killed by the police, when you type these men's names into Google's search engine the first things that come up are the videos of their deaths; nothing about their lives, who they were, who they loved, and all the things they've accomplished. All you see of them is their executions, their bodies laying on the side of road like nobody ever loved them. This constant consumption of black death on the internet and TV needs to stop. We saw Eric Garner, Sandra Bland, and so many others die on camera, the videos circulating on Facebook, Twitter and Tumblr for weeks afterward.

Ritualized black death is woven into the fabric of this nation, let's not pretend it's something new that came about because of video cameras. Police killing black people is as much a part of this country as hot dogs on the 4th of July; there's nothing new or novel about it. What seems to be forgotten is that the lynching of black people was a sport for white people during much of US history. White families, from youngest to oldest, used to watch black death as sport, often pointing and laughing. They used to sit in parks eating and laughing while watching a black person being hanged from a tree and occasionally being burned alive. Some white people would even take a picture of the event and send it as a postcard, even as Christmas cards.

An alternative to playing videos and images of black death on loop for all the world to see, is conscious, intentional, and humane reporting. In an event when a black person dies at the hands of the police, report on it. Give the readers an accurate accounting of the events; do not simply print the press releases from the police without verifying their accuracy. Do not tweet out the mug shots or "hood" looking photos of the murdered victims. Do not write extensive articles on the victim's criminal records. And do not circulate the video of the murder.

Stop taking our humanity away from us, stop leaving our bodies in the middle of a road for hours to be spectacle for onlookers. White people get to keep their humanity and dignity in life and especially in death. There are never pictures or videos of dead white people circulating social media. Mourning white families are afforded the decency of not seeing repeated images on TV of their loved ones as they die with the whole world watching.

This American sport of constantly consuming the death of black people has got to come to an end. This country needs to do better for black people and it can start with ending police violence against black people. When black people die, let it be in our old age, having lived a fulfilled and fabulous life in peace. Let it be in our homes surrounded by people who we love and who love us. Let it be in peace.

Vietnamese Veterans Continue to Feel War's Lasting Impact

by Jeff Nguyen

Every year a huge celebration for Vietnamese veterans is held in Orange County, California. My grandfather, a veteran of the Vietnam War and proud member of the Vietnamese community, watches it religiously, staring intensely at the TV set. The pride on his face is evident as the color guard marches on stage carrying a bright yellow flag emblazoned with three red stripes.

He changes the channel to watch news about Vietnam's state of affairs. Today it's a mix between President Barack Obama's recent visit to eat Pho with Anthony Bourdain and the arrests of more native journalists and bloggers, their faces forming a mosaic as the network illustrates the scale of the crackdown.

In a sense, he is still home and war hasn't ended.

∽

The Vietnamese-American community throughout Seattle and the Northwest is extensive, due in part to the Vietnam War. Through governmental and humanitarian channels, desperate and perilous escape routes, or a combination of both, many Vietnamese refugees managed to settle in the Northwest.

They included teachers, doctors, business people, and former soldiers, loyal to South Vietnam or fearing the advent of a brutal postwar occupation. Many of these former refugees, especially war veterans, are still alive today, and have interesting and powerful stories to be told.

As a person of Vietnamese descent, I was able to speak with them about their experiences during and after the war. They requested to remain anonymous because of concerns about how their stories could affect their families back in Vietnam.

Some of the veterans I interviewed were more quiet and reserved. Some were very open with their answers. All of them held one thing in common. They were all waiting for change and revolution back home. They form a part of a complex system, a Vietnam that is trying to find some identity as old regimes, capitalism, socialism and the advent of a grassroots human rights protest all collide in a bid to outline the next steps of a nation's history.

I. WARTIME

First of all, what made you decide to join the army?

INFANTRY OFFICER: "I just wanted to protect my country. It was simple. They called for volunteers as the violence began to escalate. We loved the country. We were happy to serve with so many who served alongside us. We trained together from basic, to when some of us went to officer school. There was just a lot of positivity surrounding our patriotism back then. They taught us how to fight, how to survive in the country."

VIETNAMESE MARINE: "I immediately volunteered. The Vietcong were committing numerous atrocities in their guerilla war in the south. They were an obvious threat to our communities. The marines were based on commitment and sacrifice for our community in South Vietnam. We all hated them. Soldiers in the unit hated the Vietcong with a passion. You needed to hold that hate in your heart to fight them. It was not easy."

What was the war like for you? Anxious, scared, hopeful?

INFANTRY OFFICER: "If we were scared it didn't matter. We still just had to hold on. We had to strive on. We fought alongside each other and we became brothers. We couldn't be scared. You would not be able to fulfill your job when you're scared. We saw a lot of people die. We saw it daily. I, with another soldier, carried back the bodies of the dead frequently. It was horrible but we shared our grief at least. We honored them and we respected them as they passed on. That was life out there. The feeling of how you could live or die each day ate at you."

INTELLIGENCE OFFICER: "I remember the whole division was put on holiday for Tet. We all came back to Hoc Mon and had a good time just taking a break from it all. Both sides agreed to a ceasefire during the holiday. We spent time with our families, ate and drank well, and had a breather. That did not last long. My unit holed up and prepared to defend as the Tet Offensive swept South Vietnam in '68. I remember I moved to duck behind a wall and a sniper round struck the wall just above my helmet. I cheated death. If I was simply an inch taller I would have been killed. We drove them out in a week as the American troops arrived. But what I remember most is how the other side so easily broke their promise on our sacred holiday. Despicable.

There was another instance. My unit was huddled in a trench. They started firing at us from the trees. I was directing one of my men to call in an air strike and a round hit him in the chest. He died in my arms. In the beginning the blood and death is terrifying. But at some point you become numb to it. I don't know if that's good or not. You learn to live with the grief. Raids on tunnels, uncovering weapons, I've seen Vietcong who've died to gunfire, they were maybe not even 15 years old."

VIETNAMESE MARINE: "My unit was patrolling when we were hit with artillery. It was especially fierce. And I was unfortunately hit. The shrapnel scarred my whole torso. And it had me down for a month. But I got back. And when I did, I was hit again in the exact same way. This time it hospitalized me for much longer. And I remember the commander brought me into his office. He said please have a seat. And he said, "Frankly we can't keep you out on the field in this condition, you have to accept an office job. You've been hit two times and you're still alive.""

Did you take the job?

Vietnamese Marine: "I just said no. I felt that I couldn't just sit there in an office job. I was hit two times and I still came back. Our unit was trained for fighting,we hated the enemy with a passion. I was no different. I would not sit.

I came back into action shortly after. From that, there are some memories that are buried in my mind forever. Our unit was patrolling along a dense tree copse. When we started taking fire we found the sniper who had somehow climbed to the top of a tree, and forced him to surrender. There was something about him though. He refused to put down his gun. Even after we gave him until three. I shot him in the head. He spun and fell to the ground. He died without a sound. I will never forget that single moment, for as long as I live."

II. April 30th, 1975

What was the day of surrender like?

Reserve Officer: My division surrendered on the 29th. We heard the call and we had to put down our weapons. We were just afraid for our future from then on. Where was the country was heading and what would it be like for people on the losing side? How would we be treated? Would we be incorporated back into society or would we be pariahs?

The day we surrendered, we were just assigned back to the province on guard duty. In that time, everyone was just worried. Everyone. We just were so worried. We knew were going to lose. But personally, I knew first from American intelligence sources. They told me about a month before capitulation. In that time I just wanted to go away. I could take a ship and go, but I couldn't go. I knew, but I couldn't go. I had to stay to the end. Going would betray every single value that I learned during that decade of service. So I stayed to the bitter end. And then I was sent to the camp.

INTELLIGENCE OFFICER: "I felt like a man who fell out of an airplane without a parachute on the 30th. Pure panic and fear. I remember that very well. I was scared. We fought to the furthest extent but in the end we lost. They sent assassins after me, I dug into the deepest tunnels, I interrogated the worst prisoners. But by far I remember that day the most. About a week before the surrender, I stole a jeep and took the back roads, picked up my family, and drove to Saigon, staying there until the 30th and the official surrender order. That day I had to toss my weapons into the river."

III. THE CAMPS

Can you describe the reeducation camps?

RESERVE OFFICER: "The first thing I remembered was that I was hungry. Always. There never was enough. They gave us the worst rotten rice. They cut potatoes into thin slices and dried it in the sun. We ate one cup of soup a day. We had one small bowl of rice a day. We had to work a lot. They followed us as we labored cutting down trees, clearing forests, draining wetlands, all on one bowl of rice. I was there for 6 long years.

INTELLIGENCE OFFICER: "They marked me out as a high priority threat even when I put down my weapons and basically surrendered over my lands. When I was taking my family out to the zoo, they arrested me and sent me into processing for the labor camps. Right there and then. My family was utterly shocked as I was hauled away without any warning. Over 11 years I was sent to 7 camps up and down the country. There I saw cattle and dogs getting better treatment than the prisoners. We lived on a bowl of maggoty rice a day, and labored in the hot sun to clear fields and do construction. To put it in numbers I lost about 20 kilos (about 44 pounds) in those 11 years. If it stretched on for another year I would have certainly died."

INTELLIGENCE OFFICER'S DAUGHTER: "When my father was taken away, we were left standing there in the middle of the zoo. We were never given any prior notice, trial, or charges. Those next 11 years were a nightmare.

We never received any official notice where he was going or whether he was alive or dead. He would have to write letters in secret and toss them outside the fence, where family friends would take them back to us. Mostly they said "I'm alive, please take care of yourselves." Our family would spend a whole month's salary to go to the north camps and visit him. It was a miracle how he came back to us alive after more than a decade in the camps.

IV. Post-War

Do you think we need to know and learn about this conflict? What do you think about the state of the country after the war?

Infantry Officer: "We really need to know. We need to understand what we were and how we got there. How the new regime there got to be and how they run the country. How they neglect and abuse the people. We have a role [to] reveal it for its abuses. It has lied to the point where it's not stable; people start suspecting things. The Vietnam war is an essential part of that, and of our history."

Reserve Officer: "I have hope. At some point the people will know and understand the true nature of the regime's abuses. You can see now that there are so many political prisoners in Vietnam. They all were journalists or bloggers or just people speaking out about the incessant corruption that the people are subject to. It's only a matter of time before the country changes."

Intelligence Officer: "The anxiety and the madness in the post-war regime, for me, cannot be described. They followed me constantly after I was finally released. They followed me 24/7 and I was required to report each and every activity. Groceries, taking my kids out to the park, getting coffee. I was held to a civilian trial, which I passed and I was able to come here. To this day I still am haunted by the day of surrender. I look forward to the day when it changes hands for the better, because I don't want anyone to suffer more in what that government has to offer, as I've seen too much of it during and after the war. I hope I will still be alive by then."

VIETNAMESE COLLEGE STUDENT DURING THE WAR: "I was a student during the war. My graduation was around the time that we surrendered. I felt that I became part of this lost generation. We drifted in between our old regime before the war, and the radicalization and political purge that came after. It was strange. We didn't participate in the war and didn't know what to do in the wake of all the political and social changes, although pledging allegiance to the new regime was what they told us to do. But I knew that they lied to us. They were corrupt. They delivered almost nothing they promised. Seeing Vietnamese citizens becoming more aware of the government crimes and of current events ensures that this regime will eventually fall. It's unstable, and pressures inside and outside will force a change."

INFANTRY OFFICER: "You cannot forget the Vietnamese language. Language is an essential part of our culture. Right now I keep seeing Vietnam as constantly changing. It's undergoing a shift, or it will be. Just look at China, almost the complete opposite of communist values. Vietnam is like that. It's looking for an identity. It'll take dedicated young people that want to come back and steer the country in the right direction.

INTELLIGENCE OFFICER: "Vietnamese Americans need to come back. The young people cannot ignore our country. We cannot neglect it. It will take so many people to enact a change in the country. So please don't forget your history. It is so important to know how we came about and how we ended up in this mess. Ultimately our generation will die. I want to be alive for the change, I hope that I am. But in the end it's on you to to come back and remember where you come from. Because for Vietnamese Americans, you have to know this is your 2nd country. This isn't truly where you come from. That could be in the language, the culture, and understanding the history. Never forget about your country."

THE MORE THINGS CHANGE

by Robert Zverina

It was one of those crisp, brilliant Pacific Northwest fall days that made Jim glad to be back on the mainland after two years on Maui. Yeah, Hawai'i is great, but you just don't get those kinds of days there and he missed them. Besides, the Northwest was his home and it made him feel good in a certain way that no other place ever would. It was where he was formed, its air and light bound up with his being on a cellular level.

He had to get across town to meet someone about a small job. In any other city Jim might have been an anomaly—a fix-it man with no motor vehicle. But in Seattle his car-free lifestyle choice didn't seem so strange, was even a selling point to those with Sierra Club stickers on their Subaru wagons. The barely adequate Metro bus system would take more than an hour, traffic permitting, so he opted to ride his bike, a second-hand ten speed he picked up cheap that had served him well for fifteen years. It was a perfect day for it and would probably be quicker, too.

By living frugally, Jim managed to get by working just two or three days a week. That made him something of a vanishing breed in the country's fastest-growing city. Rents were skyrocketing due to an influx of highly paid tech workaholics, which forced everyone else to work longer and harder just to keep up with the cost of living. He was one of the lucky ones. He'd inherited his parents' tiny house, one of the famed "Boeing boxes" hastily built in WW2 during a peak in Seattle's historic boom-and-bust cycle. He took a roommate and converted the garage into a rental. He preferred free time to money, but if you wanted to be a slacker in today's Seattle it helped to own real estate.

He pedaled by one construction site after another. A craftsman home that had taken a painstaking year to build and had stood intact for a century could be leveled by two men in an afternoon—one operating a rented backhoe, the other hosing down the dust. Temporary chainlink fences cordoned off deep muddy holes that would become underground garages for condos, the displaced dirt hauled off by an endless parade of grinding, belching dump trucks. He held his breath when riding by newly framed, maximum square footage shoeboxes that emanated the distinct tang of OSB—oriented strand board, the cheapest way to sheathe a building. *Good luck with that*, Jim thought, finding it ironic that the new money people would be paying top dollar to live in toxic boxes where formaldehyde and other carcinogens would off-gas from their walls for years.

The more Seattle's population grew, the lonelier Jim felt. His friends were getting priced out, quirky old haunts replaced by high end, homogenous businesses, old-timers forced to sell due to rising property taxes. Soon, there'd be nothing left. The essence of the city was evaporating fast and when the next crash came, then what? Without being consciously aware of it, his anger and frustration at this train of thought translated into faster and faster riding. He soared down a sun-dappled boulevard, making great time, way ahead of schedule. A drink would be nice, he thought, so he got off his bike. There was time.

It's possible to live a place all your life and still discover new things about it. We all get in ruts and Jim was no different. There were corners of the city he'd never visited and this was one of them, yet it still looked strangely familiar because most of it was new.

The prevailing residential style called for exterior cement board panels, cedar siding accents, and metal trim. It looked high end but in fact was the cheapest way to go. Garage doors had long since replaced front porches in these tightly packed townhouses. He noticed that with the new places, no one ever seemed to be home. He supposed that was because 90-hour work weeks were a badge of honor for those who could afford to buy in.

New office spaces were cavernous concrete hangars with dangling tube light fixtures, visible duct work, and cable-tied bundles of wire snaking above cubicle labyrinths. They looked unfinished but that no-frills corporate style was intentional, signified single-mindedness of purpose and the workers embodied that spirit, never once looking up from their screens as Jim stared in from the sidewalk, seeing if he could use his psychic powers to force eye contact with someone. After five minutes, he gave up.

It was only mid-afternoon but already the slick new restaurants were packed. The thing now was removable walls, either folding accordion-style or giant roll-downs, and all were open on this glorious day, insipid music pouring out, always a touch too loud, the patios boisterous with prosperous patrons. Jim didn't like the prices or the people. They seemed supercilious and aloof, separated from the rabble behind unsightly barriers. To Jim they resembled penned animals, prisoners of their own self-regard.

"Where's your helmet?" someone shouted from one of the cocktail corrals.

"You think I need a helmet to walk my bike?"

Well, that much about Seattle hadn't changed. Self-righteous scolds still admonished strangers minding their own business. Jim held up his messenger bag, to which he'd strapped his helmet. He felt stupid for doing it, for even having acknowledged the busybody, but by then the guy had turned his attention elsewhere.

Jim tried to stay positive but it was getting harder to do. He could deal with the city changing, but he was afraid how those changes might change him. He'd been raised in the quasi-zen non-dogmatic agnostic Buddhist Northwest tradition and continually reminded himself that reaction to antagonism was just another form of attachment. At 6'4" and 220 pounds, his friends regarded him as a gentle giant, little suspecting what a struggle it was for him to keep his naturally short temper in check.

He was imagining what a pleasure it would be to smash that jerk in the face with his helmet when he saw The Scupper. It stood out like a soiled bandage. A little sliver of a bar, blank brick façade with just one small window, minimal signage, unchanged since the time when morality codes dictated discretion and patrons were permitted to drink only when sitting down. It looked good to Jim. Like a way out. An escape from the tawdry uniformity that was swallowing his city.

Jim was old enough to remember the time before cell phones and flat screen TVs, when a neighborhood bar was where you went to hear the latest gossip or fall into philosophical conversation with someone you just met. There were few like it left and it gave him hope to find this hidden gem. He smiled at the metal bucket of sand outside the door, empty itself but surrounded by cigarette butts as if the smokers had deliberately missed. Classic.

Stepping inside was like descending into a storm cellar, seeking shelter in a musty, unfamiliar place. After his eyes adjusted, he saw it was a relic from the days when outlying neighborhoods were still forests and big timber was as much a nuisance as a resource. There was so much lumber then they used it more like building blocks than framing. The walls were solid 2×4, stacked against each other like books on a shelf; the high ceiling was similar, 2x6s or 2x8s or maybe even 2x10s, laid on edge and pressed against each other, bomb-proof as a concrete bunker.

Everything was wood. Wood floors and wood booths and an ornate curved wood bar with neo-classical wood pediments holding up a wavy wood-framed mirror. Wood shelves, wood doors, wood moulding, wood stools, and a wooden bartender standing wordlessly, arms folded, looking superior and bored. The only splash of color was the disarranged dots of an abandoned pool game, green felt faded under hooded light. There was a small TV at one end of the bar, mercifully off.

It was quiet. No music playing, no clatter of dishes in some unseen kitchen. A worn-out woman twisted on her stool and smiled at Jim as he came in, then nervously looked back down at her clear drink. Jim took the thin, grey-haired man at the far end of the bar for the owner. With his tight haircut and trim moustache, he looked like an ex-cop. He had a half-empty Miller gone flat in the bottle and never looked up from his crossword puzzle, just continued muttering clues to himself, working the boxes with a pencil, cursing with every erasure.

The counter had been rubbed by generations of elbows, stained black from contact with decades of skin, infused with ten million exhalations of nicotine and tar. Smoking was prohibited now but there was still a subtle undertone emanating from the porous walls. A yellowed poster of the Kingdome hung above the antique cash register, showing the season schedule for the inaugural '77 Mariners.

Jim plopped down squarely between the two barflies, three vacant stools to either side. He set his bag down on the one immediately to his right.

Mr. Crossword looked up, sour. "Someone might want to sit there."

Jim made light of it. "We'll burn that bridge when we come to it."

He ordered a beer and nodded at the poster, said to no one in particular, "Thirty-eight years later and they still haven't made it to the World Series. How do you win 116 games and not go all the way?"

The woman came to life. "I know! What year was that?"

"2001."

"Yeah, well, that's when my husband finally gave up on them." She stirred melting ice with her straw. "He died a year later. I'm Sandy."

"Jim. Pleased to meetcha. The 1906 Cubs won 116 games. *They* made it to the World Series, but lost. Maybe 116's an unlucky number?"

Mr. Crossword put down his pencil. "Baseball—who cares?"

Jim had to admit he didn't really care either, not since the '94 strike ended up canceling the whole season, but he enjoyed the tradition of it. "When I think of baseball, it's in black and white."

The bartender, silent until now, said, "Interleague play is what ruined it for me. What's the point of a World Series if the two teams already played each other earlier in the season? I like soccer now. More action, anyway."

"Yeah, but no suspense," Jim said.

"You have to know how to watch it."

"No thanks."

"My husband always said, 'Baseball is a game, not a sport.' Maybe that's the difference?"

"Can we change the subject?" Mr. Crossword folded his paper and pocketed his pencil in disgust. He turned to the weather page and muttered to himself, "Where is it not hotter than 80 but never snows?…"

Jim, ever friendly, asked, "Looking for paradise?"

"Aren't we all?"

"Eighty and never snows? Sounds like Hawai'i, though it does snow above 10,000 feet. If you're looking for paradise, I'd say that's it."

"Not for a white man."

Jim kept himself in check. After two years there, he saw it not as the 50th state, but an occupied nation. He supported the sovereignty movement and saw this guy with his dull pencil as everything wrong with the tourists and carpetbaggers who saw the natives as either picturesque servants or inexplicably surly threats.

"Ever been there?"

"Like I said, it's no place for a white man."

"In a way, you're right," Jim said archly, but the man missed his point.

"You know where it's not too hot and almost never snows?"

"I can't wait to find out."

"Right here! Seattle!"

"It does get cold, though."

"I didn't say I never wanted it cold. I just don't like it too hot, and I don't like snow. Hasn't snowed here in years. Where you from?"

"Seattle."

"No, I mean where were you born?"

"Seattle."

"Yeah, well my grandparents were born here. Both of 'em."

"Only two grandparents? I guess people were a lot closer in those days."

"You're damn right they were!"

It got quiet again until Sandy, noticing Jim's bike helmet, changed the subject.

"I have a client who's so afraid of the Next Big One she keeps a helmet by her bed and bottled water in every room. She carries that helmet with her all over the house. I think she sleeps with it on. She was in that big California quake—"

"The one that interrupted the World Series?" the bartender interrupted.

("Baseball again," mumbled Mr. Crossword.)

"That's right. San Francisco."

"I'd rather not live in that kind of fear. In that case it might be better to be oblivious."

"There's fear and then there's knowledge," Crossword said.

"Fair point," Jim conceded.

"Oh, my teeth hurt!" Sandy said as she finished her drink, implying it was for medicinal purposes as she ordered another double gin and tonic.

"So, go to the dentist," Crossword said. "What's the matter—you afraid?"

"I don't mind the drill; it's the bills that scare me."

"My friend got his work done in Thailand," Jim said. "Worked out cheaper even with airfare and hotels than getting it done here."

"Yeah, if you want to trust your life to a Third World country," Crossword sneered.

"I dunno. He said their equipment was more up to date than what he's seen here and crowns didn't cost a thousand bucks a shot."

"I couldn't get away from work, probably," she sighed. "What kind of bike you got?"

"Nothing special, just an old 10-speed."

"I used to have one. French."

"Mine's French—Motobecane."

"I gave it away. Just left it on the curb and in five minutes it was gone. I just got too scared riding in the street."

"It's only getting worse. More cars, more distracted drivers."

"My husband got doored. That's not what killed him. Broke his collarbone, though. That's when I quit."

"My girlfriend got doored," Jim said. "She wasn't hurt but she got knocked into traffic. Luckily, the cars stopped in time."

"Probably their fault," Crossword said.

What was it Jim had read? People who upset you are really there to teach you? He tried to keep things civil, saw this as a chance to enlighten the misinformed.

"Not according to law. There's precedent. It's the driver's responsibility to look before opening their door."

"Not in my book. It's simple—most of you guys are assholes."

Jim sat very still. To look at him you'd never have guessed the effort it took. He asked, dead flat and level, "Are you the owner of this bar?" After all, he figured, a man's entitled to express his opinions, no matter how ignorant, in his own bar.

"Thank God, no."

"Well, I don't like what you're implying. You got more to say?"

Jim didn't know what he'd do next, only that it hinged on what the man said next.

Somewhere, a bird flew into a window. "Naw, it's time for me to go."

Jim untensed, half sorry for this peaceful resolution. "You won't be missed."

The man left some bills on the bar and stepped to the bathroom. As soon as he was out of earshot, Sandy leaned close and stage-whispered, "That's Frank—he's an asshole!"

"That much is obvious." There was no joy or promise in Jim's last gulp of beer.

When Frank came out he offered Sandy a ride home. Despite what she'd said, she accepted. That left Jim alone with the bartender, who talked about wanting to move to Arizona because a former governor had had the balls to rescind MLK day.

"Gee, that doesn't sound racist at all."

"That's not what is was about. Don't get Frank wrong. He's an asshole, but the best kind."

"The man's a bigot."

There wasn't much more to say after that, from either side.

Jim looked around and felt more alone than ever.

～

In the parking lot, Frank and Sandy talked across the hood of his Cherokee.

"Jesus Christ, Frank! Are you crazy? Did you see the size of that guy? He was ready to kick your ass!"

"Don't I always know when to pull back?"

"But why do you do it? What fun is it pissing people off?"

"Guys like that have it coming."

"Guys like what?"

"I don't know. I can just tell."

"One of these days you're gonna push the wrong guy too far."

"Not as long as I've got back-up." He pulled the pistol from nowhere.

"I wish you wouldn't carry that."

"I've got a permit."

"I don't like it. And I'm not getting in with you unless you unload it."

"Sure, babe. Anything you say. You're always safe with Frank."

He dropped the magazine out of the grip and pocketed it, forgetting there was still a round in the chamber—a common error. Then he tucked the gun into his waistband and shot his dick off.

No one would miss it.

Except him.

I Don't Care That You Pissed Us Off, BLM, Thanks for Doing It!

by Andrew Lanier

Waiting in line to see Bernie Sanders rally at the Alaska Airlines arena, I get a text about the rally at Westlake: the Black Lives Movement took over the stage and wouldn't let Bernie speak. My gut reaction is annoyance and anger; why did they shut down Bernie's rally? Don't they know he's the candidate most likely to actually address the issues they care about? Why didn't they pull that kind of stage-hijacking stunt at a Donald Trump event? I say as much to my wife, disgustedly. She listens without saying anything, looking at me. *Maybe there's something more to it than what you know?* Indeed, there is.

"Welcome to the Bus!" We find our seats after an oddly warm greeting from the Metro driver, noting a few people holding Bernie Sanders signs on the way to the rally at UW. Up front, someone's liberal grandparents are discussing the candidate's various policies with a toothless woman who is obviously delighted to see the event. "I want to know his position on Palestine," grandpa says. I double take—he's a dead ringer for Bernie. The toothless woman tells him, "I hope I don't offend you, but you look just like Bernie Sanders! But with better hair." He chuckles and everyone laughs. Discussion ensues on the hairstyles of various candidates, with special mention of a famous politician's $500 haircut a few years back. Who was that again? "John Edwards," pipes the guy a seat back. The mood is jovial, anticipatory. In front of me sits an orange corduroy suited man with dyed, thinning hair seemingly inspired by Weird Al Yankovic and a rainbow troll doll. He observes that Donald Trump's hair "looks like an animal died on his head." I whisper something snarky to my wife about glass houses and throwing stones. She winces, says nothing. The bus driver peppers in commentary, asking the Bus is they are excited to see the rally. Whoops and applause. Then, he leads the Bus in a chant of "Bernie, Bernie, Bernie!" He is excited too. Rolling up to the stop outside Husky Stadium, he bids us goodbye and clarifies, "For the record, as an employee of Metro King County, I hold no personal opinion and maintain completely neutrality on all political matters." Laughter spills out of the bus as we disembark. Amidst the discussion of hair and Palestine, of course, nobody mentions Black Lives Matter.

Regarding BLM, when you believe your cause to be of dire urgency while your continued shouts remain unheard, you have to resort to an extreme measure. That measure must be taken amidst the very people who are most likely to support your cause, even if it pisses them off.

Streams of progressive peoples coalesce into a line stretching from the Alaska Airlines arena around Husky Stadium, those of us the BLM movement called useless in supporting racial justice. Ouch. Signature gatherers swarm the line, "Have you signed our petition to reduce climate change? Do you support rent control?" Heading into the arena, I wonder what Bernie will say about race.

Climbing the stairs into the upper tier, we find our seats. Rather, they find us. A middle-aged liberal mama bear waves us over, "Y'all need some seats? We got two right here." Settling in, I overhear the discussion with her friend, "You hear about that guy from the bottled water company who said everyone should have to pay for drinking water? Asshole. I'd punch em in the face if I ever saw em." Glancing over, I smile. "Oh, I'd do it, too, don't you doubt that." Over her glasses, her look assures me she would, indeed, do just such a thing. Thus, we are introduced to Marian. The arena fills to the rafters, sweltering with 12,000 bodies, all waiting. Needing water, I wonder if the concession stands take credit cards. Marian pulls a twenty out of her wallet, "Here, honey, buy whatever you want." Humbled, I accept. Returning, she tells us she worked in a correctional facility for a spell and is disgusted by what the drug war is doing to this country. We discuss politics further. I show her statistics I had pulled for my previous article on the Republican debate, noting how infrequently the candidates mentioned the poor, income inequality, and race compared to illegal immigration, Obama, and war. She shakes her head, disgusted. "Those mother*****s. I better stop. I'm gonna get myself in trouble." I remark, jokingly, that I doubt she ever gets in trouble. "Honey, I get in trouble all the time! Listen…" She tells us that she works for a regulatory agency locally that recently concluded an investigation to shut down a retirement home for neglect and abuse. Apparently, in a meeting discussing what the legal repercussions would be for the man responsible, she suggested, "We oughta just shoot em. And that's why I can't say the word 'gun' at work anymore." She throws up her hands.

Back to BLM, in prisons across the country, a disproportionate number of black people languish under drug sentences that exceed the likely penalty that man will receive. A traffic stop or a confrontation over selling loose cigarettes can end in death. What will Bernie say to address this?

Finally, the introductory speakers hit the stage, each greeted with crackling excitement and the hail of 24,000 hands clapping together. They don't need to fire up the audience; merely set them loose. Each statement is concluded with a riot of support, drowning out the speakers at every instance before they can move on. A clear theme runs through their speeches: Black Lives Matter. Each speaker nails it from a different angle; the crowd roars in approval. The president of the Washington Labor Council punches it out with authority: "We know we have to commit to justice. Black Lives Matter."

Symone Sanders is introduced as the national youth chair of the Coalition on Juvenile Justice, and as of today, the campaign's new national press secretary. She is a huge presence, commanding the stage and belting out her speech. Arena-shaking applause follows each of her statements. "Michael Brown, Eric Garner, Tamir Rice, Sandra Bland, Trayvon Martin, Walter Scott, Freddie Gray, Rekia Boyd…!" She lists their names and others, the names of the black lives that have galvanized the Black Lives Matter movement and shook the nation. "Michael Brown, Eric Garner, Tamir Rice, Sandra Bland, Trayvon Martin, Walter Scott, Freddie Gray, Rekia Boyd." Naming them again, she softens to mention there are countless other names we have never heard. "Black. Lives. Matter!" She stamps out this imperative; the crowd thunders in confirmation. She is booming; she absolutely radiating energy and hope and passion; she is also black. I think to myself, this woman is a star.

Bernie takes the stage. The arena explodes. "BERNIE! BERNIE! BERNIE!" From the nosebleed seats feet stomp in a rolling drumbeat that reverberates through my chest.

Amidst his calls for addressing economic equality, providing free college tuition, getting big money out of politics, and all the other progressive darlings, there it is: "No president will fight harder for racial justice than I do. Period." He lays out his case for ending mass incarceration (Marian whoops), bolstering the Voting Rights Act, ending the war on drugs, ending mandatory minimums, enacting federal jobs programs to combat the high rates of unemployment that black youth face, among others.

Hugely, the next day, before a rally in Portland, Bernie Sanders' campaign puts forth a comprehensive statement detailing his racial justice platform, which is aimed at combating, "the four central types of violence waged against black and brown Americans: physical, political, legal and economic."

The Black Lives Movement pissed off and inconvenienced some people in Seattle who went to the Westlake rally and waited hours to hear Bernie speak. So what? Black people in America have waited centuries to have their grievances heard and addressed. The rhetoric of the protestors is distasteful to many people, who don't like being called useless false liberals and part of a racist system. So what? When a candidate like Bernie Sanders calls for policies like ending mass incarceration, they'll cheer and support for it, as they should.

Back in the arena, Bernie is closing and it's a fever pitch revival. My wife and I, Marian, the girl on my left screaming me into early hearing loss, and 12,000 other people from Seattle are all standing and clapping and stomping together to hear the words of a man we believe can change the country. We hear his message, his words, and the words thrust forward by two black women hours before at Westlake. And we agree: Black Lives Matter.

THE GAS-LIGHTING OF A NATION

by Lola E Peters

There's been a lot of chatter on social media about gas-lighting lately. The concept is taken from the 1944 movie, Gaslight, about a woman whose husband slowly manipulates her into believing that she's going insane. He does this by convincing her, time and again, that events she experiences are just figments of her imagination. He isolates her from friends and family, persuading her that it's for her own good. She keeps saying that the gaslights in their house are flickering at night. He tells her it's in her imagination. In fact, he is the one causing the lights to flicker while he is searching for jewels in the attic of that house where he killed the woman's aunt decades earlier.

On social media, the conversation is about relationships and how some people use gas-lighting to avoid taking responsibility for their own actions. Let's explore how this works. Mary is being gas-lighted by her husband, John. For example, he has convinced her that his infidelity was caused by what he calls her "over-emotionalism." Mary then tries to be less emotional. John accuses her of being cold and unfeeling. Mary becomes more emotional, and round and round it goes. John then makes an appointment with a therapist for Mary. He tells the therapist that Mary is an emotionally manipulative woman and he needs help saving his marriage. In her first session, Mary cries uncontrollably, reinforcing John's statement.

So why bring this up now, as we celebrate the birth of Dr. Martin Luther King, Jr. and the strides of the Civil Rights Era? Think about it. What greater example do we have of gas-lighting than the way people of color have been treated in this country?

A group of European Christians land on this continent. They brutally kill millions of indigenous people with no thought of their humanity. How do they justify this? They call the indigenous people "savages" then, despite proof otherwise, they claim the native people have no religion or culture. Next, they drag Africans across oceans in chains, throwing those who rebel into the sea, and somehow still convince themselves and the world that they are "the good guys" and that people of color, especially those of African descent, are the ones who are insane and morally deficient.

For six centuries these Europeans and their progeny tell this story, never seeing their own savagery, never taking responsibility for the murder and mayhem they perpetuate. Then they take this same attitude towards the rest of the world. They justify invading islands, countries, and peoples from Hawaii to Iraq using this same gas-lighting technique. They shift money from providing education, health care, and economic stability to creating weapons for war and facilities for incarcerating those in the society with the least resources. Yet somehow they manage to convince their citizens that "We're Number One" all the while other countries are soaring past them in education, health care, and economic stability.

We are told that black people don't do well in school, inferring that we're not very bright. Yet without Dr. Charles Drew's method for separating plasma from blood, millions of people around the world would die every year, and without Vivien Thomas millions of babies born with heart defects would die before their first birthday. We are told that black people don't do well with money, yet when we built our own, successful, separate economy because we were excluded from the general economy, our communities in Rosewood, FL and Greenwood, OK were destroyed by rioting whites. We are told we don't have the ability to think complex enough thoughts to become scientists, engineers, or mathematicians, yet the gas mask that has saved millions of lives during war was invented by Garrett Morgan. And then there's Neil de Grasse Tyson... need I say more?

The gas-lighting has become so ubiquitous that few people even question it. Even some people of color have absorbed the lies. Why else would someone like Bill Cosby make derogatory statements about black children's names while not wincing at the names Amadeus or Yuri or Rhys or Gwyneth?

People of color on this continent have been saying that the gaslights are flickering for generations. Dr. King and the Civil Rights movement brought the flickering to the attention of the nation. For a brief time, the nation saw the truth. Then Ronald Reagan and his cronies began blaming African Americans for the conditions in which we were trapped. After denying us access to education, jobs, and housing, they blamed us for having substandard education, finances, and housing.

It has taken us decades to begin to recover. Black Lives Matter has brought attention to the gaslights again. Again we see the likes of Donald Trump and others who hold all the resources and want to blame us for not having them. Bankers make the rules for financial access, pull the rug out from under millions of homeowners, and then blame us for falling flat on our faces.

The purpose of gas-lighting is to accrue power. The first step toward recovering from gas-lighting is refusing to believe the lie. It's telling the truth regardless the consequence. And it's holding others accountable, refusing to believe their lies just because they "look like such nice people." People who seek to steal our power do not have our best interests at heart. Before sharing our power with anyone, labeling them a leader or spokesperson, we need to be sure they have earned it and will not abuse it.

We need to call out the lies and the liars. We need to stop believing the story of our brokenness and deficiency. We have survived six centuries of European rule on this continent because there are those, like Dr. King and Ella Baker and many others who refuse to believe the lies told about us. Who are, in fact, proof that those are lies.

And we must never forget, we are on indigenous land. We stand on the land of the Duwamish people. People our federal government says don't exist, yet are evident everywhere we look. We must refuse to be gaslighted. When confronted with blanket racial statements, we must ask these questions:

- How is this different from the reality of white people (e.g.: do white people do drugs)?

- What are the real statistics (e.g.: most crime in the Puget Sound region is committed by white people. To quote President Obama's 2016 State of the Union address, "Food Stamp recipients didn't cause the financial crisis; recklessness on Wall Street did.")?

How can we change our internal dialog so that the questioning becomes natural? Ask one question: what if it was me, or my loved one. What would I do if a police officer beat my brother or violently arrested my grandfather? What would I do and want others to do if someone randomly shot my child to death because they didn't like what they were wearing? Instead of offering sympathy, go inward and explore empathy. Stop needing to be innocent and "the good guys" and explore being the humane one. There is no true justice without empathy, without the understanding of our own flawed humanity and, by extension, everyone else's. From there we can rebuild our society in a way that's sustainable. Otherwise, make plans for our collapse because the current path of fractured self-interest will lead us to our own extreme Balkanization and eventual destruction. We have the chance to choose, but that window of opportunity will not be forever open.

How can we best celebrate Dr. King? Choose today to make that change. Play the long game: exchange empathy for the short-term strategies of winning.

Our Continued Rise Up The Mountaintop

By Marcus Harrison Green

The following is a transcription of a speech delivered by Marcus Harrison Green at Mount Zion Baptist Church in Seattle on Friday, January 15, 2016.

When they first asked me to speak here today, and said they wanted me to answer the question of whether society had reached Martin Luther King's "mountaintop of racial harmony," I'll have to be honest. My initial reaction was that these people have got to be crazy if they think this speech is going to last any longer than three seconds.

But after realizing I was expected to deliver more than one syllable, the question really got me thinking deeply. It actually took me back to a day seven years ago, to the last day of my grandfather's life.

I never ever dreamed a day like this was possible.

January 20, 2009. I remember it vividly. To me that day was the height of what it meant to be black in this country, the day I thought we reached that mountaintop—that was certainly the mood at the time. It was the day an African-American man finally strolled with his family down Washington's Pennsylvania Avenue to get sworn in to the highest office in this nation.

Cloud nine wasn't high enough for me that day—I was on cloud infinity to the fifth power, and what made it sweeter, what made it even more memorable, was that I shared it with my grandfather. He had been debilitated by a heart condition for months, but on that day he got up the strength to watch the inauguration.

My grandfather Jimmie Green was not an emotional man. Growing up, I never once believed he was capable of shedding a tear. But that day he couldn't help but be overcome with joy, the type of joy that only comes when you finally see something that for so long you've been told is impossible.

And so I asked him—I asked this man who had grown up a share-cropper in a segregated Arkansas; who, because of the laws at that time, was forbidden from going beyond an eighth-grade education; who had been called "boy" so long it took him until his late twenties to fully believe he was a man; who wasn't allowed to fight for this country in a segregated military, but was allowed to cook for the soldiers who did; and who couldn't cast a vote for a president until he was 35—I asked my grandfather if he ever thought a man who looked like the one he voted for that November could ever become president.

"No," he answered. "No, I never ever dreamed a day like this was possible."

"But, Marcus," he cautioned, "be careful, because as good of a day as this is, it's just one, and we need many more. We still have higher to rise."

That's the last thing he ever told me. Later that night he fell into a coma and passed away, having seen the impossible.

But his words always stuck with me, though they were hard to process at first.

It was difficult to not be seduced by the notion that our society had finally vanquished its race problem. That we had now ushered in a golden era of "colorblindness."

It was difficult to not be seduced by the notion that our society had finally vanquished its race problem.

It's hard, almost impossible, for us to not be seduced by the pervasive assumption that we are more than 90 percent of the way to racial utopia. Somehow we are supposed to believe that this nation's history—one of genocide, slavery, suppression, and exclusion—cannot possibly impact the present or future. That blatant acts of racism are now few and far between, relegated to the margins of simple-minded militia members in western Oregon or the bloviating, fascist presidential candidates they lovingly support.

We can point to the room that has been made for people of color and women at the top of our society's totem pole, their high visibility in positions of power.

We can point out that explicit forms of racism have been on the wane since MLK spoke of his mountaintop. No more are there police dogs that ravage the bodies of marchers; no more are there billy clubs that fracture the skulls of protesters, or water hoses to impede their progress. No more signs to designate where we can or cannot be seated or served.

I hear that racism is dead from some of my own black brothers when discussing the case of Sandra Bland, the woman mysteriously found dead in her prison cell after a routine traffic stop, or the case of John Foster, killed within seconds of Ohio police arriving to a Wal-Mart for holding a BB gun.

Many of them—long conditioned to what they call "proper" interaction with law enforcement—tell me Bland and Foster should have known to mind their behavior in front of an officer. That ultimately the duo is responsible for their own deaths.

I hear tales of racism's demise so often from my liberal white brothers and sisters, who spout that the true culprit is a crisis of culture, a lack of personal responsibility, and a chronic condition of moral malaise.

I hear of its end in the midst of a society whose black infants are three times more likely than white infants to die within the first months of birth, despite no biological deficiency.

I hear racism is a relic in a society that mocks the provision of safe spaces for its marginalized students while actively creating safety for those it values.

No, racism is not exclusively overt as it once was. What it is now is sophisticated.

I read racism's obituary even after a recent reporting trip, when a white mother told me that she could never know what it was like to suffer in the same way that a black mother does in this country, because if her 12-year-old child was to be killed by a police officer, her son's murder would be a crime.

Racism is not dead. It is just like the Greek hydra, that beast that regenerates in a new form just as you've begun to celebrate its defeat.

No, racism is not exclusively overt as it once was. What it is now is sophisticated. What it is now is systemic.

For every Bettie Jones, needlessly killed by Chicago police responding to a dispute she had nothing to do with, it creates a million Yvettes who will die early deaths because they are economically bound to an area with limited access to healthcare.

For every Trayvon Martin, there will be a million Andres swallowed whole by a criminal justice system that will never offer a chance for redemption. That will forever brand them with a scarlet F for felon. Their lives, now absent of opportunity, will be nothing more than slow deaths.

As it was once housed prominently in the hearts of unrepentant bigots, racism stubbornly finds shelter in the institutions of our society and that society's systems.

The gears of these systems continue to be greased with black bodies, and function regardless of the good intentions of the men and women pulling the lever. It does not matter whether the hands of the people holding that lever are black, as they are in the city of Baltimore, or if those hands are white, as they are in Ferguson, Missouri.

Nor does it matter if they are brown, or beige, or metallic marble.

The outcome is always the same: mass devastation of black life.

So, are we there yet? To ask the question in this country is to answer it.

To consider your life in context is not a demonstration of weakness, but an exhibition of character.

The racism we encounter today can't be solved by old efforts nor a civil rights-era understanding of what we face. In truth, we can't even entertain the question of "are we there yet" before answering a more important one: Where are we now?

That question is tougher, because we occupy different planes of existence in this country, and so we must be honest about our social locations. Because you can only know what direction to go by knowing exactly where you stand.

What guides us to those locations is a word that is so misused and cheapened by that misuse.

Love.

When I say the word, I say it as one that equates to the resiliency needed by those who fight for racial justice, with seemingly no avail, to the point that their knuckles are raw and bleeding, and yet they must continue to fight.

I say that word that is synonymous with the acceptance necessary by those bestowed advantages, whether because of pigment or class. Who must see past fragility and privilege and realize that to consider your life in context is not a demonstration of weakness, but an exhibition of character.

When all groups who have been discriminated against in this country sit down to eat at America's dinner table, it's love that asks them to understand that when they see a race that has been malnourished for so long pleading to feed on America's promises, that race is not insisting that all others should starve—they are just trying to eat like everyone else.

I say love in a way that translates to faith, the faith required of all of us. Faith in that what so often goes unseen in our human brethren. Faith in their capacity to change, their capacity to grow.

That word, and the deeds it inspires, is the only way I know to change this world. This world we live in by choice, and, yes, our collective circumstance is a choice.

We can live in the world as we were born into, or we can live in the world as it can be.

I know that last point causes cynics to grind their teeth. They think this world we live in is the best of all possible, that our present is as good as it can possibly be. But this world in its present state is constructed by no laws of nature. It is built on a foundation of ideas, beliefs, and doctrines of people, and kept in place by our fear, apathy, and resignation.

And it can only be undone by the new ideas, imagination, and beliefs of other people.

We can live in a society that puts a higher value on some lives, or we can choose to live in a society where all lives truly matter, including black ones, but we cannot have both.

We can live in the world as we were born into, or we can live in the world as it can be.

This world as it can be isn't one left to fantasy, or one that only exists in dreams, no matter how noble. It is one being birthed right here, right now.

It is being birthed in this city of Seattle by Devan Rogers, a Seattle Central student. A young woman who couldn't tolerate that, in this liberal bastion she calls home, more than half of all incarcerated juveniles were children of color, so she helped get that same city to pass a resolution to move toward the goal of zero-percent youth incarceration and an alternative to imprisonment.

It's birthed right here in this county named after Martin Luther King Jr. by Bridgette Hempstead, who couldn't sit back any longer and abide the continuous health disparities found in unincorporated King County's Skyway area. Because of her effort, its mostly poor black and white population will soon have access to health services long denied them.

It is birthed right here in this state of Washington by Dominique Davis, who was sick and tired of burying black, brown, red, and poor white youth, and is working to install violence prevention and racial sensitivity training in every school district in this state.

Respectively, they are a student, a semi-retired mother of three, and a part-time football coach. These people hold no elected office, and they more than likely will never have a national holiday in their name.

They are people who possess nothing more than empathy, courage, resolve, and conviction.

They are people who embody Dr. King's legacy, a man who in all his reverence, in all his glory, was still just a man. A man who was as flawed and as human as we all are today.

Sainthood is not a requirement for progress.

I say that not to injure his legacy, but to truly do it justice. Because that legacy tells me that sainthood is not a requirement for progress. It doesn't matter one iota if you are fractured, broken, or bruised, because your participation in this world is mandatory to transform it.

His legacy tells me it doesn't matter whether your position is the president of the United States or a Starbucks barista between dream jobs. Whatever your occupation, when you fight against hatred, you propel justice.

His legacy tells me that no matter how dark our days, there will be light. There will be hope. There is hope today, because we all woke up this morning. You woke up this morning with courage, conviction, and empathy at your disposal, the raw ingredients to heal this sick world, if you just choose to activate them.

That legacy tells me that there is no measure too small in our ascent up to Dr. King's mountaintop. So in a climb that no one person, no one generation, will complete alone, his legacy tells me it doesn't matter whether the actions you take to combat racial madness are measured in centimeters, inches, or feet. For our society, there are no insignificant steps upward.

Dr. King knew this when he told us in his last speech that he wouldn't get there with us. My grandfather knew this when he told me we still had far to go. I'll know this someday long from now, when my granddaughter asks me, "Grandfather, are we there yet?" and I'll tell her then the same exact thing that I'll tell you now.

I'll say to her we've climbed far, but we have farther still to rise, so now go reach up and pull us higher. You rise up and you pull us higher.

Acknowledgements

⌒

Marcus Harrison Green would like to thank all the exceptional poets, artists and writers who contributed work to this anthology. He would also like to thank Third Place Press for their generous financial and time contributions in ensuring the creation of this book.

Green also expresses gratitude to all past and present *South Seattle Emerald* Board Members: Devin Chicras, Bridgette Hempstead, Seferiana Day, Maia Segura, Dominic Smargiassi, Andrew Johnston, and Dominique Scalia.

A hearty thank you also to those who have helped steward the *Emerald* since its inception: Sonya Green Ayears, Mark Baumgarten, Sarah Stuteville, Mark Newton, Susan Gleason, Daniel McCrea, Dustin Washington, Alex Garland, Dominque Davis, Paul Nelson, Matt Mills McKnight, Karen Toering, Greg Hanscom, Phillip Green, Tamara Power-Drutis, Mary Goebel, Jessica Partnow, Susan Davis, Michael Charles, Alex Stonehill, Anne Althauser, Gregory Davis, Jenny Frankl, Beau Hebert, John Helmiere, Senait Brown, Morgan Wells, Emily Williamson, Donna Nickelberry, Ben Hunter, Teri Youngman, John Helmiere and Cynthia (Mama)Green.

Appreciation also to Eric McDaniel of Third Place books for initiating this anthology.

Thank you also to the long-suffering Vladimir Verano whose dedication and hard work made *Emerald Reflections* a reality.

Last but not at all least, Green cannot thank his beloved community of South Seattle enough.

About the Editor

MARCUS HARRISON GREEN, is the co-founder of the South Seattle Emerald, a former Reporting Fellow with *YES!* Magazine, a board member of the Western Washington Chapter of the Society of Professional Journalists and a recipient of Cross Cut's Courage Award for Culture.

Growing up in South Seattle, he experienced first-hand the neglect of news coverage in the area by local media, which taught him the value of narratives.

After an unfulfilling stint working for a Los Angeles based hedge-fund in his twenties, Marcus returned to his community determined to tell its true story, which led him to start the *South Seattle Emerald.*

The publication has become a go-to source of community information in a part of the city that rarely receives much press outside of the police blotter. As he says "The media spends so much time talking about the death here, that it rarely ever talks about the abundance of life also found here."

Green sees storytelling, particularly journalism as democracy's most essential tool. He says its function is not only to speak truth to power, since the powerful most often already knows the truth, which is usually why they try to hide it.

Journalism's true job, he says, is to speak truth to the many who believe they are powerless; it reminds them they aren't.

He is proud to live in the "South End" of Seattle.